THE WASHINGTON
ADVENTURE

Ruth Pelz

Gibbs Smith, Publisher

Published by
Gibbs Smith, Publisher
P.O. Box 667
Layton, Utah 84041
800-748-5439
www.gibbs-smith.com/textbooks

Managing Editor: Susan Allen Myers
Associate Editors: Aimee L. Stoddard, Courtney J. Thomas
Assistant Editors: Ryan Carr, Jennifer Petersen, Carrie Gibson
Photo Researchers: Ruth Pelz, Susan Myers, Aimee Stoddard, Carrie Gibson

Book Designer: Robert Holman
Maps and Graphs: Robert Holman

Cover photo: Chuck Place, *Hoh Rain Forest*, Olympic National Park

Printed and bound in China
ISBN 0-87905-986-9

10 09 08 07 06 05 04   10 9 8 7 6 5 4

This book is dedicated to
the teachers who use it. Your
dedication inspires us all.

ABOUT THE AUTHOR

Ruth Pelz has been writing textbooks and other educational materials for more than twenty-five years, including Washington State and western history books for elementary and secondary students, teachers guides, and interactive science and culture curricula. She currently is Education Planner for the Burke Museum of Natural History and Culture.

ABOUT THE EDITOR

Susan Myers works with historians, reading specialists, authors, editors, and artists to publish quality history textbooks for elementary and secondary students. She has produced sixteen state history text-books for schools across the country.

ABOUT THE REVIEWERS

Robert Carriker, Ph.D., has been teaching American history at Gonzaga University in Spokane for over thirty-five years. He has authored and edited numerous books and articles on western history, including subjects such as Lewis and Clark, the Columbia River, Jesuit missionaries, and Native Americans.

Kraig A. Schwartz, Ph.D., teaches U.S. history and the history of the Pacific Northwest at Seattle Central Community College. His special area of interest is late nineteenth and early twentieth century social history. He has contributed to many journals and books, including *Washington in the Pacific Northwest* for secondary students.

Orlan Svingen, Ph.D., teaches American history at Washington State University in Pullman. His special interest is American Indian history. He has published many articles and books on the native groups in the West.

Contents

Maps

State Symbols

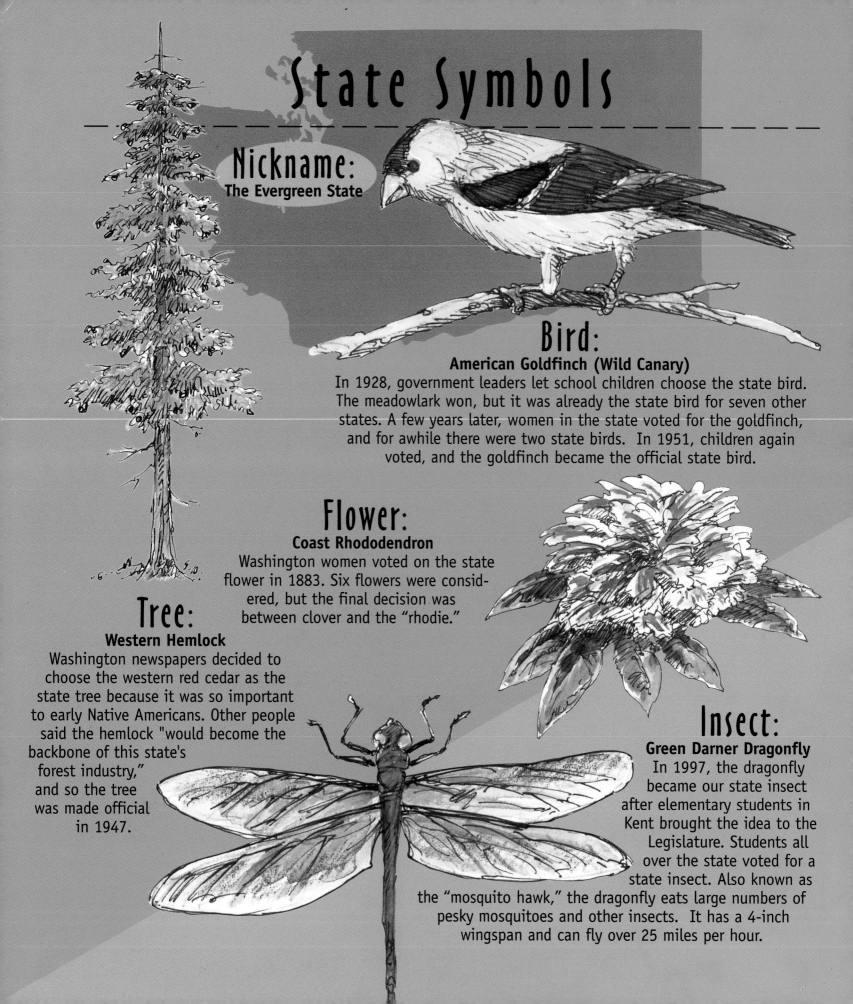

Nickname:
The Evergreen State

Bird:
American Goldfinch (Wild Canary)
In 1928, government leaders let school children choose the state bird. The meadowlark won, but it was already the state bird for seven other states. A few years later, women in the state voted for the goldfinch, and for awhile there were two state birds. In 1951, children again voted, and the goldfinch became the official state bird.

Flower:
Coast Rhododendron
Washington women voted on the state flower in 1883. Six flowers were considered, but the final decision was between clover and the "rhodie."

Tree:
Western Hemlock
Washington newspapers decided to choose the western red cedar as the state tree because it was so important to early Native Americans. Other people said the hemlock "would become the backbone of this state's forest industry," and so the tree was made official in 1947.

Insect:
Green Darner Dragonfly
In 1997, the dragonfly became our state insect after elementary students in Kent brought the idea to the Legislature. Students all over the state voted for a state insect. Also known as the "mosquito hawk," the dragonfly eats large numbers of pesky mosquitoes and other insects. It has a 4-inch wingspan and can fly over 25 miles per hour.

Fish:
Steelhead Trout

Steelhead trout is one of the most popular fish for sports fishing. It is an anadromous fish, which means that it returns to spawn at the same place in fresh water where it began life. It became our state fish in 1969.

Fruit:
Apple

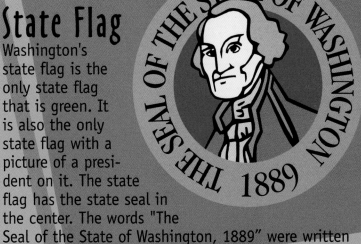

In our centennial year, 1989, the apple was named a state symbol. During World War II, dried apples were shipped to soldiers overseas. When the war ended, Washington farmers had too many apples. Soon they started making frozen apple juice and planted different kinds of apples that were popular for eating. Candy was made from apples, too. Apples are one of the most recognized symbols of the state.

Dance:
Square Dance

When pioneers came west, they brought with them a dance called the quadrille, which means square in French. Dancers are directed by a caller, and turn and move to the tune of fiddle music.

Fossil:
Columbian Mammoth

In 1998, students from an elementary school near Cheney led the effort to have the mammoth voted our state fossil. The mammoths ate grasses and other plants. They lived about 65 years. Males were about the size of modern elephants, and females were smaller. Nearly all mammoths died out about 10,000 years ago.

State Flag

Washington's state flag is the only state flag that is green. It is also the only state flag with a picture of a president on it. The state flag has the state seal in the center. The words "The Seal of the State of Washington, 1889" were written around the seal. What happened in 1889?

THE SEAL OF THE STATE OF WASHINGTON 1889

State Song

The song became official in 1959.

Washington My Home
Helen Davis, arranged by Stuart Churchill

This is my country; God gave it to me;
I will protect it, ever keep it free.
Small towns and cities rest here in the sun,
Filled with our laughter. Thy will be done.

Chorus:
Washington my home; Wherever I may roam;
This is my land, my native land,
Washington, my home.
There's peace you feel and understand,
In this, our own beloved land.

We greet the day with head held high,
And forward ever is our cry.
We'll happy ever be,
As people always free.
For you and me a destiny; Washington my home.
For you and me a destiny; Washington my home.

▲ Olympic National Park photo by LaVelle Morris

▼ Columbia Gorge photo by Barbara Murray

State Folksong

The song was voted as the state folksong in 1987.

Roll On, Columbia
Woody Guthrie

(Yes) Roll on, Columbia, roll on,
Roll on, Columbia, roll on.
Your power is turning the darkness to dawn,
Roll on, Columbia, roll on.

Now other great rivers add power to you,
Yakima, Snake, and the Klickitat too,
Sandy, Willamette, and Hood River too,
It's roll on, Columbia, roll on.

Tom Jefferson's vision would not let him rest.
An empire he saw, the Pacific Northwest.
Sent Lewis and Clark, and they did the rest.
It's roll on, Columbia, roll on.

At Bonneville Dam there are ships in the locks.
The waters have risen and covered the rocks.
Shiploads of plenty will steam past the docks.
So roll on, Columbia, roll on.

And far up the river is Grand Coulee Dam,
The mightiest thing ever built by a man,
To run the great factories and water the land,
It's roll on, Columbia, roll on.

What is our state's largest river? What river forms a natural boundary with Oregon? What river produces the most electricity for the state? If you answered the Columbia River to all three questions, you were right!

Photo by Chuck Pefley

Natural Washington

chapter 1

Lesson

1

Where Are We?

PLACES TO LOCATE
North America
Canada
Mexico
Oregon
Idaho
North Pole
South Pole
Columbia River

**WORDS TO
UNDERSTAND**
continents
country
degree
equator
geography
hemisphere
latitude
longitude
prime meridian
symbol

THE LAND WE CALL HOME

Washington State seems very large. Yet it is just one small part of the world. Because we live in Washington, it is important to us. It is our home. People all over the world live in places that are important to them.

In this chapter you will begin to learn about Washington by studying its *geography.* You will learn where Washington is located in the world. You will study Washington's land and waterways. You will learn about the plants and animals that live here. You will see how people in Washington live and how they are connected with people all over the world.

Why is it important to know about the geography of a place? Because geography affects where we live and how we live.

WHERE IS WASHINGTON?

We all know we live on Earth. But just where on Earth do we live? Washington State is located on one of the world's *continents.* Continents are very large land areas. They have oceans on many sides. Washington is on the continent of North America.

Washington is part of a *country* on that continent. A country is a land region under the control of one government. Our country is the United States of America. Canada is the country to the north of us. Mexico is the country to the south of us.

Relative and Exact Locations

There are many ways to describe the location of a place. **Relative location** tells where something is in relation to other things. For example, Washington is north of Oregon. It is south of Canada. It is between Idaho and the Pacific Ocean. In the same way, you could tell someone that you live near the Columbia River, or next to the school, or down the hall from your friend's apartment.

Exact location tells exactly where to find a place. An address is an exact location. You might say, "I live at 405 River Street, in Richland, Washington."

Where in the World Are We?

1. *Our **world** is the planet Earth.*

2. *Our **continent** is North America.*

3. *Our **country** is the United States of America.*

Canada

United States

Atlantic Ocean

N
W E
S

Gulf of Mexico

Mexico

Pacific Ocean

4. *Our **state** is Washington.*

Canada

Washington

Montana

Oregon

Idaho

LINES AROUND THE WORLD

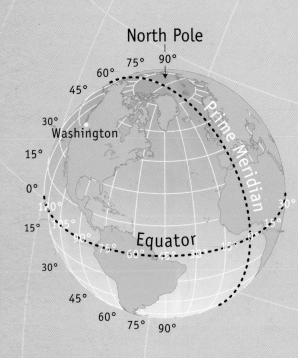

Every place in the world has an exact location that is measured by *latitude* and *longitude* lines. You can find these lines on a map or a globe.

Latitude lines run east and west (side to side on the map).

Longitude lines run north and south (up and down on the map).

Along the lines you will find numbers. Each number has a tiny circle by it. This is a *symbol* for a *degree*. A degree is a part of a circle or globe.

The degree numbers all begin at 0. The *equator* is 0 degrees latitude. Find the line that is 0 degrees longitude. It is called the *prime meridian.* Find these lines on the globe. The degree numbers get larger as they move farther away from the equator and the prime meridian.

Activity

Where Is Washington?

On this map, find Washington's **latitude** lines of 49° North and 46° North. Use a globe in your classroom to trace these lines all the way around the world.

1. Which **longitude** line is near the western border of Washington State?

2. Locate about where you live on the map. What is your longitude and latitude?

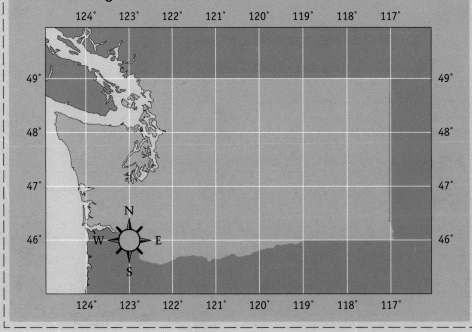

Hemispheres

There is another way we divide up the earth. We pretend that the earth is cut into two equal pieces. We call each half of the earth a *hemisphere*.

Look at these drawings of the earth. Find the equator. Find the hemisphere north of the equator. Find the hemisphere south of the equator. Since north is nearly always "up" on a map, it's not hard to guess that the hemisphere north of the equator is the Northern Hemisphere. What is the hemisphere south of the equator called?

Now, what if we decide to divide the earth another way? Geographers often divide it from the North Pole to the South Pole. The line runs through the Atlantic and Pacific Oceans. This drawing shows a Western Hemisphere and an Eastern Hemisphere.

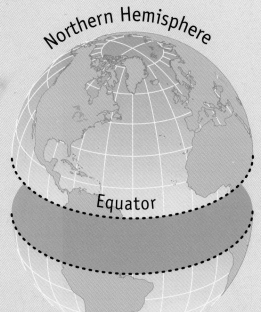

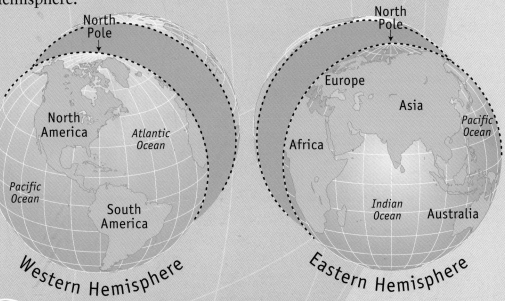

Memory Master

Lesson 1

1. Name four things that are part of the study of geography.
2. Describe Washington's location in at least two ways.
3. What country is south of the United States?
4. Do latitude and longitude lines on a map help us find exact or relative locations?
5. What are the four hemispheres?

▲ Which things in this picture are human features?

What Kind of Place Is Washington?

PLACES TO LOCATE
Northwest
Puget Sound
Columbia River
Columbia River Gorge

WORDS TO UNDERSTAND
conserve
freshwater
generator
human feature
hydroelectricity
natural environment
natural resource
pollute
tide
transportation

▲ Marina photo by Shirlee Simon-Glaze

▲ Photo by Sunny Walter

Deer roam the beach at Olympic National Park. Sandy beaches, rocky coastlines, and wild animals are part of our natural environment.

OUR NATURAL ENVIRONMENT

The people of Washington State are lucky. We live in a beautiful place. Our state has towering mountains and gently rolling hills. We have sandy beaches, rocky coastlines, deep lakes, and sparkling rivers. We have forests, meadows, grasslands, and many wild animals. All of these things are part of our *natural environment.*

Places also have **human features.** They include cities and towns, roads and airports, farms and factories. Homes, schools, and shopping centers are human features, too. Humans make all these things.

MANY NATURAL RESOURCES

Natural resources are things found in nature that people use. Washington's forests are a good example. Many people in the state have jobs cutting down trees, sawing logs into lumber, or making things from wood. Wood is used to make homes and other buildings. So are gravel, stone, and cement.

Salmon, crabs, and other seafoods are also natural resources. Rich soil for farming is a resource; so are rushing rivers. Our beautiful mountains, waterways, and islands are a resource, too.

It is important to protect our resources so that they will still be here for people in the future to use and enjoy.

What natural resources provide jobs where you live?

Many people in the state have jobs cutting down trees, sawing logs into lumber, or making things from wood.

PEOPLE USE AND CHANGE THE LAND

People change the natural environment in many ways. They cut down forests. They plow fields to plant crops. They build dams and bridges across rivers. They dig into the ground to get silver and gold.

These changes can be important. They provide things we all need such as homes, food, roads, and jobs. However, these same changes sometimes harm the environment.

There was a time when people thought they could never use up all the salmon, trees, and other resources of the Northwest. They thought there would always be plenty of fresh air and clean water. It wasn't true. Cars and factories *polluted* the air. As cities grew, the natural homes of many plants and animals were destroyed.

Then the people of our country began to understand how important it is to use resources wisely. They passed laws to help stop pollution of the air and water. They set aside some land for parks and wildlife. Today, people are working together to keep our state a good place to live.

You Can Help

It is up to everyone to help *conserve* natural resources and protect the environment. You can help. Never litter. Recycle cans and paper. Turn off lights and televisions when you aren't using them.

You can help prevent forest fires by being careful with campfires and matches. Everyone can help take care of Washington.

A Place by the Water

▲ Columbia Gorge photo by Barbara Murray

Water has always been important to the people who live here. Look at the map of Washington cities on page 36. How many of them are located near a river, bay, or other body of water?

Most of them! Can you guess why?

Water Is Important for Transportation

Before there were cars, trains, or airplanes here, boats were one of the main ways to get from one place to another. Today, large ships and smaller boats carry things in and out of our harbors and up and down our large rivers. Water *transportation* is still important today.

Water Is a Source of Food

Fish, oysters, clams, crabs, and mussels are examples of foods from the salty sea. Fish also live in our *freshwater* lakes, rivers, and streams. Our most important fish—salmon—lives part of its life in freshwater and part of its life in the ocean.

Rivers Help Make Electricity

As river water rushes through dams, it makes electricity. Inside a dam are giant machines called *generators.* As water flows down through the dam, it makes the generators turn. This produces electricity. Electricity made by water power is called *hydroelectricity.* The Columbia River is the state's largest river and its most important source of electricity.

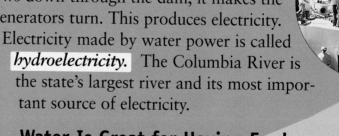

Ship photo courtesy of The Port of Seattle ▲

Water Is Great for Having Fun!

Of course, oceans, rivers, and lakes are also great places to play! Swimming, sailing, boating, windsurfing, and fishing are popular water sports here. How do you like to have fun in the water?

◄ Photo by Will Baker

The Washington Adventure

Nooksack River

Ross Lake

Methow River

Columbia River

Okanogan River

Pend Oreille River

Skagit River

Sanpoil River

Strait of Juan de Fuca

Soleduc River

Lake Chelan

Lake Crescent

Snoqualmie River

Banks Lake

Roosevelt Lake

Spokane River

Wenatchee River

Quinault River

Hood Canal

Puget Sound

Cle Elum Lake

Yakima River

Columbia River

Moses Lake

Palouse River

Gray's Harbor

Puyallup River

Naches River

Chehalis River

Nisqually River

Willapa Bay

Snake River

Pacific Ocean

Cowlitz River

Klickitat River

Lewis River

Columbia River

N
W   E
S

0   100 Miles

Scale of Miles

Ocean Tides

If you have been to ocean beaches, you know that the water level changes during the day. These changes are called **tides.** During high tides, the water comes high up on the beach. Then the tide goes out and the water level falls. This low tide is a good time to see crabs and starfish and other sea animals. Look in pools of water in the beach rocks.

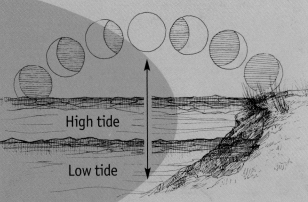

High tide

Low tide

When the moon is full, the high tide is very high and the low tide is very low. Between the full moons, the tides are not quite as high or low.

Lesson 2

Memory Master

1. Name at least four natural resources of Washington.

2. What are four ways that water is important to the people of Washington?

3. What is one thing that you can do to protect the natural environment?

Our Climate

WET OR DRY?

Climate is important to a place. Climate is what the weather is like year after year. The amount of rain or snow that falls each year is part of the climate. The usual number of hot days in summer and cold days in winter are part of climate, too.

Washington's climate has an interesting story. The story begins far out over the Pacific Ocean. As air passes over the ocean, it picks up *moisture.* Wet ocean winds blow over Washington from west to east.

When the air reaches the mountains, it must rise. As air rises, it cools, and cool air cannot hold so much moisture. Then the water falls to earth as rain or snow. As a result, western Washington gets a lot of *precipitation.* Some coastal areas get almost 150 inches of rain each year.

By the time the winds reach the other side of the Cascades, the air has very little moisture left. This is why the eastern parts of the state are much drier than the western side. Some parts of eastern Washington are deserts. They receive less than 10 inches of rain a year.

The ocean affects our climate in another way. Large bodies of water change temperature more slowly than the air does. The ocean helps keep nearby places cooler in summer and warmer in winter. This is why western Washington has a milder climate than eastern Washington does.

▶ Olympic National Park photo by LaVelle Morris

▶ Eastern Washington sagebrush photo by Mike Green

What is wind? Wind is moving air. Air moves when it is heated or cooled. Warm air rises. Cold air sinks. This movement makes wind.

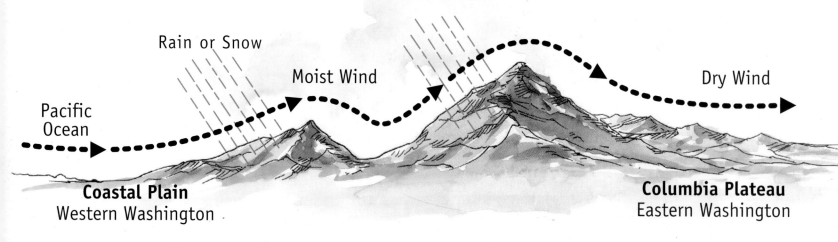

Rain or Snow

Moist Wind

Dry Wind

Pacific Ocean

Coastal Plain
Western Washington

Columbia Plateau
Eastern Washington

◄ Part of our state is near the ocean, and is wet most of the time. The air feels moist. It rains often. In this picture, a trail wanders through the rain forests of Olympic National Park.

Part of our state is separated from the ocean by tall mountains. It is too dry for dense forests to grow. Sagebrush grows wild on the driest lands. What wild plants grow where you live? ▼

Natural Washington

CLIMATE ZONES OF THE WORLD

There are many things that affect climate. The most important is distance from the equator. The sun shines more directly on places near the equator. Lands near the equator have a hot climate.

The lands farthest from the equator are cold all year long. These lands are close to the North and South Poles.

The lands in between are not always hot nor always cold. The United States is between the equator and the North Pole. It has both hot and cold weather.

Climate and Elevation

Elevation also affects climate. Elevation means how high the land is above the level of the ocean. The *average* level of the ocean is called *sea level*. It is the starting point for measuring elevation.

Washington has both low land and high land. Parts of the coastline are just a few feet above sea level. Mt. Rainier is the highest point in the state.

The higher you go, the colder it gets. Our highest mountains are covered with snow all year.

The wet and mild climate of western Washington is called a *marine climate*. Marine climates are near an ocean.

Eastern Washington has a dry *continental climate,* with hotter summers and cooler winters. Why is this true?

How are climate and weather different? Climate is the big picture, year after year. Weather is what we get each day. Each day's weather can be sunny or rainy, warm or cold, windy or calm.

Mt. Rainier is the highest point in the state. It is 14,410 feet high.

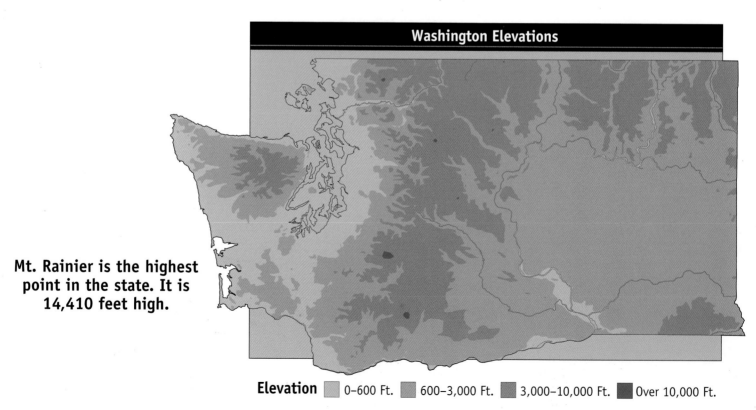

Washington Elevations

Elevation ▢ 0–600 Ft. ▢ 600–3,000 Ft. ▢ 3,000–10,000 Ft. ▪ Over 10,000 Ft.

Habitats

Habitats are the natural places where certain kinds of plants and animals live. There are several kinds of habitats in Washington State. Here are some of them.

Coastline

The land along the coasts is full of life. Fish, seals, and other animals swim in the coastal waters. Kelp, seaweed, and sea grasses grow there. Clams and geoducks live in the sea bottom. Many kinds of birds live near the shore.

Temperate Rain Forest

Not all rain forests are in tropical climates! Washington has rain forests, too, with tall spruce, hemlock, and cedar trees. Smaller plants grow on the forest floor. Some areas have trees that are hundreds of years old. These special places are called **old growth forests.** They are home to many animals, including spotted owls, other birds, and lots of insects.

Alpine Meadow

High on the mountains, it is too cold for trees to grow. Alpine meadows are covered with snow most of the year. In the short summer season, the meadows are filled with flowers. Animals of the alpine habitats include mountain goats, sheep, cougars, marmots, and smaller animals such as chipmunks and pikas.

Sage Steppe

Compared to the rain forest, the dry lands of Washington seem empty. However, many plants live here. One is the sagebrush, which gives this habitat its name. Other shrubs, grasses, and a few small trees grow, too. Animals such as pronghorns, skunks, raccoons, coyotes, rodents, and snakes live in the dry climate.

What is your favorite kind of apple? Washington farmers grow many kinds.

The Washington Adventure

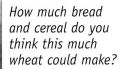

◄Canola and barley grow side by side. Canola is used to make cooking oil. Barley is a grain used in soup and other products.

How much bread and cereal do you think this much wheat could make?

FARMS AND GARDENS

In many places of Washington, the natural *vegetation,* or plant life, is hard to find. Grasslands have been replaced by wheat farms. Much of the old growth forest has been cut down. In the cities, parks and gardens often have the only plant life you can see.

A lot of plants grow well in the wet climate of western Washington. Peas, berries, and flower bulbs are among the important crops.

In the dry lands on the other side of the state, many crops need extra water in order to grow. Many farmers use sprinklers to *irrigate* their crops. The important crops include apples, pears, cherries, grapes, potatoes, and wheat. Farms are the biggest business in many eastern parts of the state.

Flowers are an important crop.

Lesson 3

Memory Master

1. Describe the climates of eastern and western Washington and tell why they are different.

2. How does distance from the equator affect the climate of a place?

3. How does elevation affect the climate of a place? Which lands are colder—those with a high elevation or a low elevation?

4. Name one habitat of Washington and name at least one plant and one animal that live there.

Lesson 4

Landforms

LANDFORMS

Look at the shapes of the land around you. What do you see? Are there mountains and valleys? Are there hills or plains? All of these natural features are *landforms.* Even bodies of water such as rivers and lakes are sometimes called landforms. They are part of the shape of the land.

See how many of these landforms you already know. Then see how many of the others you can learn.

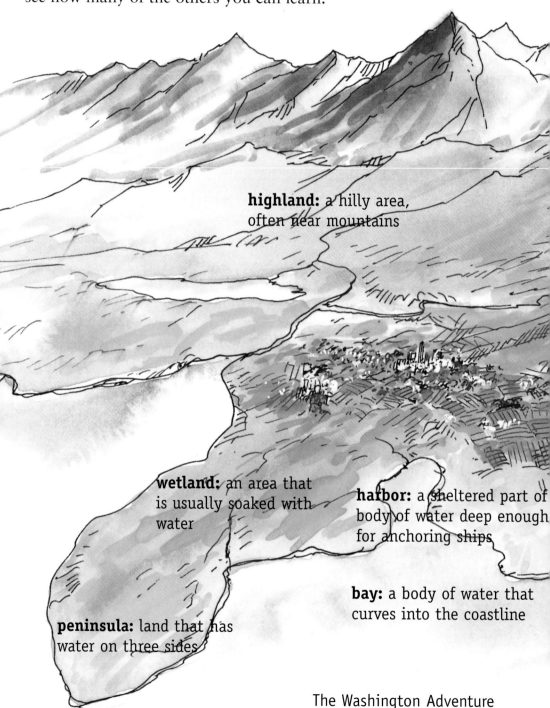

highland: a hilly area, often near mountains

wetland: an area that is usually soaked with water

harbor: a sheltered part of body of water deep enough for anchoring ships

bay: a body of water that curves into the coastline

peninsula: land that has water on three sides

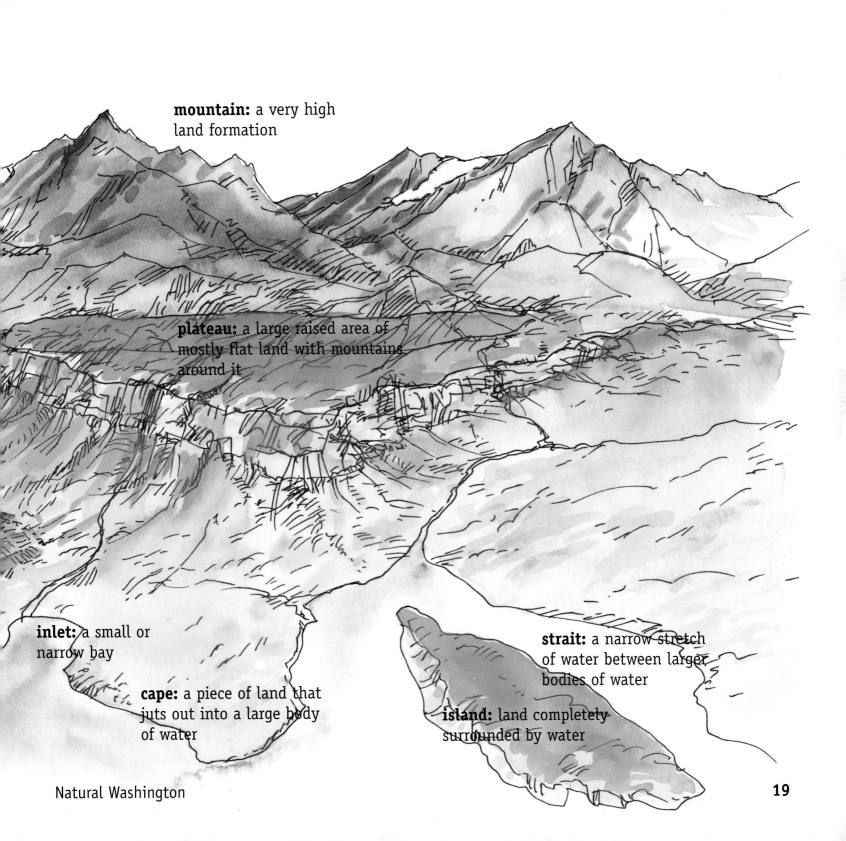

mountain: a very high land formation

plateau: a large raised area of mostly flat land with mountains around it

inlet: a small or narrow bay

cape: a piece of land that juts out into a large body of water

strait: a narrow stretch of water between larger bodies of water

island: land completely surrounded by water

Natural Washington

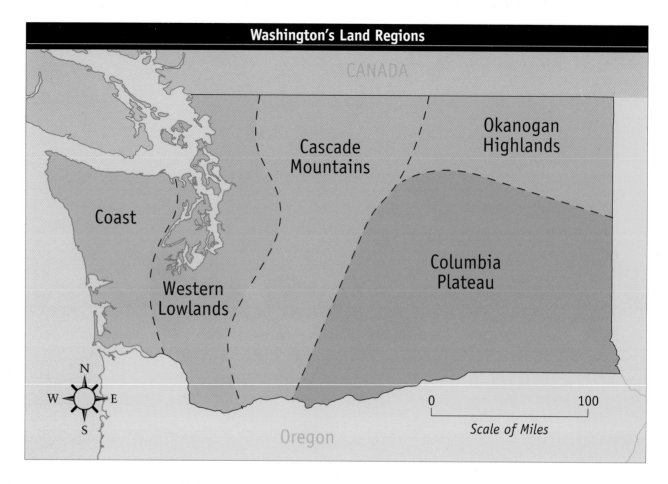

WASHINGTON REGIONS

Regions are places that are alike in some way. They are another way to divide up the land.

A region can be as large as a continent or as small as your neighborhood. You can live in many regions at the same time. For example, if you live in the Yakima Valley, you are in a desert region. You also live in an important farming region.

Land Regions

If you were a bird flying over the land, you would see five different kinds of land. That's a lot for just our state! These five areas are the *land regions* of Washington. Their names give clues to the main landforms of each region.

- Coast
- Western Lowlands
- Cascade Mountains
- Columbia Plateau
- Okanogan Highlands

The Washington Adventure

Coast

Washington's coastal region is the wettest part of the state. Some parts of the coastline are rough and rocky. In other parts there are wide sandy beaches. The elevation varies from sea level up to the snowy peaks of the Olympic Mountains. Coastal, alpine meadow, and rain forest habitats are all found in this region.

▼ Olympic Mountains photo by Chuck Place   ▶ Photo by Tom Till

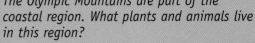

The Olympic Mountains are part of the coastal region. What plants and animals live in this region?

A starfish lives in the tidepools at Olympic National Park. Tidepools are left when the tide goes out.

Boats come in and out of Seattle's downtown harbor.

▲ Photo by Mary Levin

Tacoma is a busy city. What mountain do you see?

Western Lowlands

This region of river valleys and low hills surrounds Puget Sound and the Cowlitz River. The climate is mild and damp. Forests once covered most of the land, but today the region is full of cities, towns, and farms. Seattle, Tacoma, Olympia, and many other cities are located here. There are many harbors for large ships and small boats.

▲ Photo by Chuck Pefley

The Washington Adventure

There are many great places to camp in the Cascade Mountains.

Cascade Mountains

These tall, rugged mountains divide the eastern and western parts of our state. Winters are long and cold, and the summers are short. The west side of the mountains has thick forests and a wet climate. It gets lots of rain and snow. The eastern slopes are drier, and the forests are more open.

Columbia Plateau

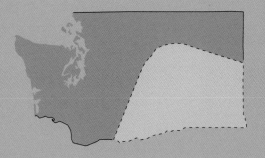

This region includes the driest land in Washington. It also includes some of the most valuable farmland in the state. Irrigation brings river water to farms. Our sagebrush steppe habitats are found here. There are also large areas of grassland and scattered trees. Spokane is the largest city in this region. There are other cities along the Columbia, Snake, and Yakima Rivers.

▼ *Can you see why this place is called Dry Falls?*

▼ *Spokane is the largest city in this region.*

▲ Dry Falls photo by Dale Straddling

▲ Photo by Chuck Pefley

▲ Photo by Chuck Pefley

The Columbia Plateau includes some of the best places in the country to grow wheat and other grains.

The Washington Adventure

There are no large cities in the Okanogan Highlands region, but there are small towns and cattle ranches.

Okanogan Highlands

This region of steep hills and river valleys is sometimes called the Okanogan Highlands. It is part of a much larger region called the Rocky Mountains. The Rockies are the largest mountain range in North America. Forests cover some of the highlands. There are no large cities here, but there are small towns and many ranches. To make a living, people farm, raise cattle, and cut timber.

What do you think?

Why do you think most people in Washington live in the Western Lowlands and not on the Columbia Plateau or in the Okanogan Highlands?

Natural Washington

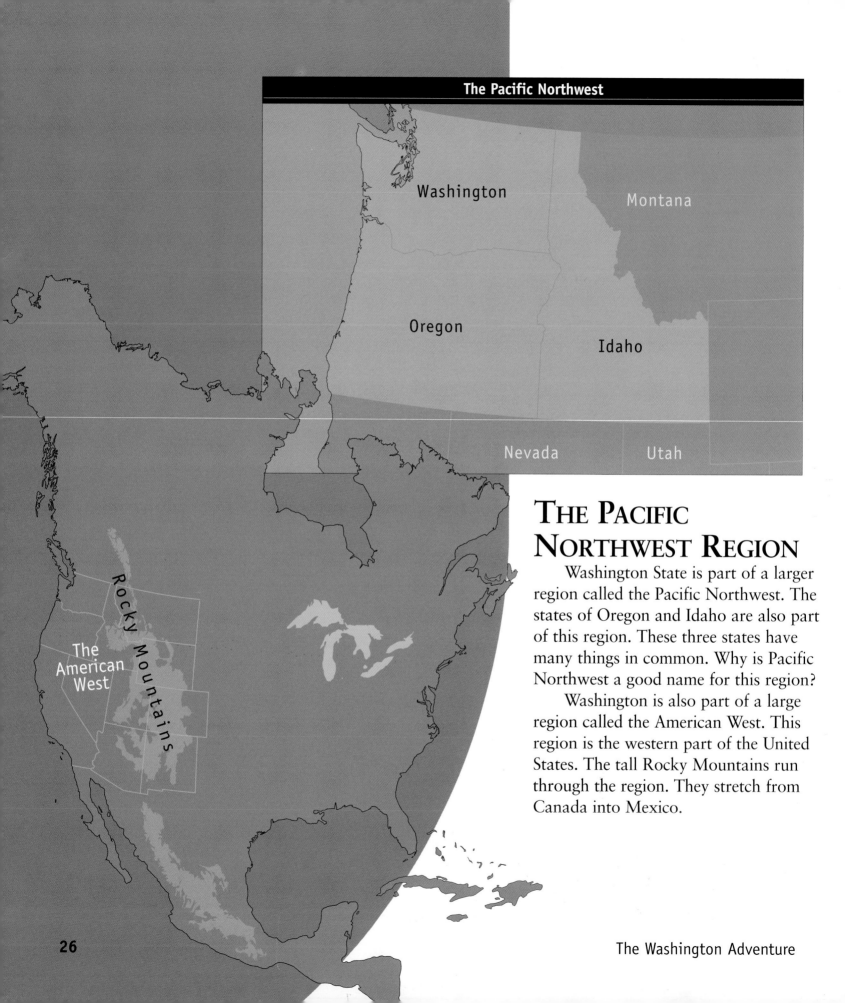

Washington

Montana

Oregon

Idaho

Nevada

Utah

Rocky Mountains

The American West

THE PACIFIC NORTHWEST REGION

Washington State is part of a larger region called the Pacific Northwest. The states of Oregon and Idaho are also part of this region. These three states have many things in common. Why is Pacific Northwest a good name for this region?

Washington is also part of a large region called the American West. This region is the western part of the United States. The tall Rocky Mountains run through the region. They stretch from Canada into Mexico.

The Pacific Rim

Find the Pacific Ocean on a globe or world map. Then find Washington State and all the other lands that lie on the edge of this ocean. These lands make up a large region called the Pacific Rim.

Japan, China, Korea, and other countries in Asia all lie along the Pacific Rim. The United States and many other countries are part of the Pacific Rim, too.

Each day, ships and airplanes travel between the cities of the Pacific Rim. They carry people and products back and forth. Visit a busy port city in Washington and you will see examples. You may see a ship bringing cars from Japan. You may see Washington farm products being loaded and shipped to China. You may see airplanes full of tourists and business people. All of this *trade* with countries of the Pacific Rim is important to our state.

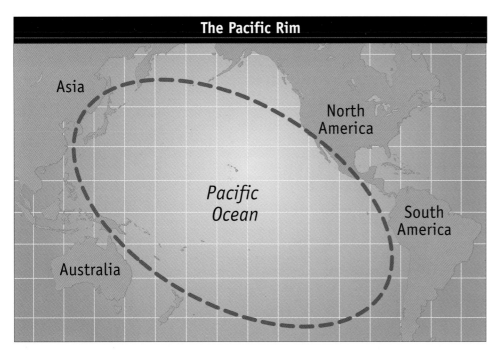

The Pacific Rim

Asia

North America

Pacific Ocean

South America

Australia

Lesson 4

Memory Master

1. List the five land regions of Washington and tell a little about each one.
2. In which land region in Washington do most of the people live?
3. Name three larger regions of which our state is a part.

Fossils are remains or traces of *ancient* plants or animals in rock. When geologists study fossils, they learn about life long ago. These palm fossils tell us that Washington used to have a much warmer climate than it does today.

THE CHANGING LAND

The landforms around us seem to stay the same forever. But *geologists* know that our land was quite different long ago. Geologists are scientists who learn about the history of the earth by studying rock and landforms. Some study fossils. Others study valuable *minerals* that are found in rocks. Geologists also study *earthquakes* and *volcanoes* to help keep our homes and cities safe.

Washington State is a great place to study *geology*. There are wonderful fossils here. There are some unusual landforms. There are many interesting stories in the history of our land.

Lava Covered the Land

One unusual story began about 17 million years ago. Where Washington, Oregon, and Idaho come together today, cracks opened up in the earth. Hot melted rock called *lava* began flowing out of the cracks. As the lava cooled, it shrank and cracked.

This happened over and over again. In many places, the lava was hundreds of feet thick. Rock that was formed this way can be seen in large areas of the Columbia Plateau.

Did you ever wonder if dinosaurs lived here? Geologists don't know the answer! The lava flows are one of the reasons. Lava covered the dirt and rock that were here in dinosaur times. If there were any footprints or bones left behind, the lava covered them up.

▲ Photo by Ruth Pelz

Layers of basalt can easily be seen in Palouse Canyon. Basalt is rock that was once lava.

Scientists have found fossil skeletons of saber-toothed cats. This is one of many large animals that lived here during the Ice Age.

WASHINGTON IN THE ICE AGES

About 2 million years ago, the earth's climate began to grow colder. Huge sheets of moving ice, called *glaciers,* formed at the north and south poles and began to spread.

These cold periods are called Ice Ages. During the last Ice Age, glaciers covered the northern part of Washington.

As these glaciers moved, they carved great valleys and scraped off the tops of hills. Puget Sound was mostly carved out by Ice Age glaciers. So were Lake Washington and Hood Canal.

About 10,000 years ago, the Ice Ages ended. The climate got warmer. Water from melting glaciers caused great floods. These floods carved out Palouse Canyon and the Grand Coulee and formed the rough "scablands" in the center of the state.

That's Thick!

Ice was about 5,000 feet thick over the place where Bellingham is today. It was 4,000 feet thick over the place where Seattle is today. It was only 1,800 feet thick over the Tacoma region.

When the glaciers melted, the water spread over the land and formed rivers and lakes. Today's city of Spokane was covered by a lake over 500 feet deep.

Pacific Ocean

Washington

Ice Age lake

Oregon

During the last Ice Age, glaciers covered northern parts of Washington.

Legend

Edge of the ice sheet

The Washington Adventure

During the Ice Ages, the rich soil of the Palouse Hills was formed. Fine ash from volcanoes and dust from the ground was blown for miles until it settled on the ground. Ice Age flood water also brought rich soil to the Palouse. This happened over and over again until soil up to 150 feet deep covered large regions of rock.

Natural Washington

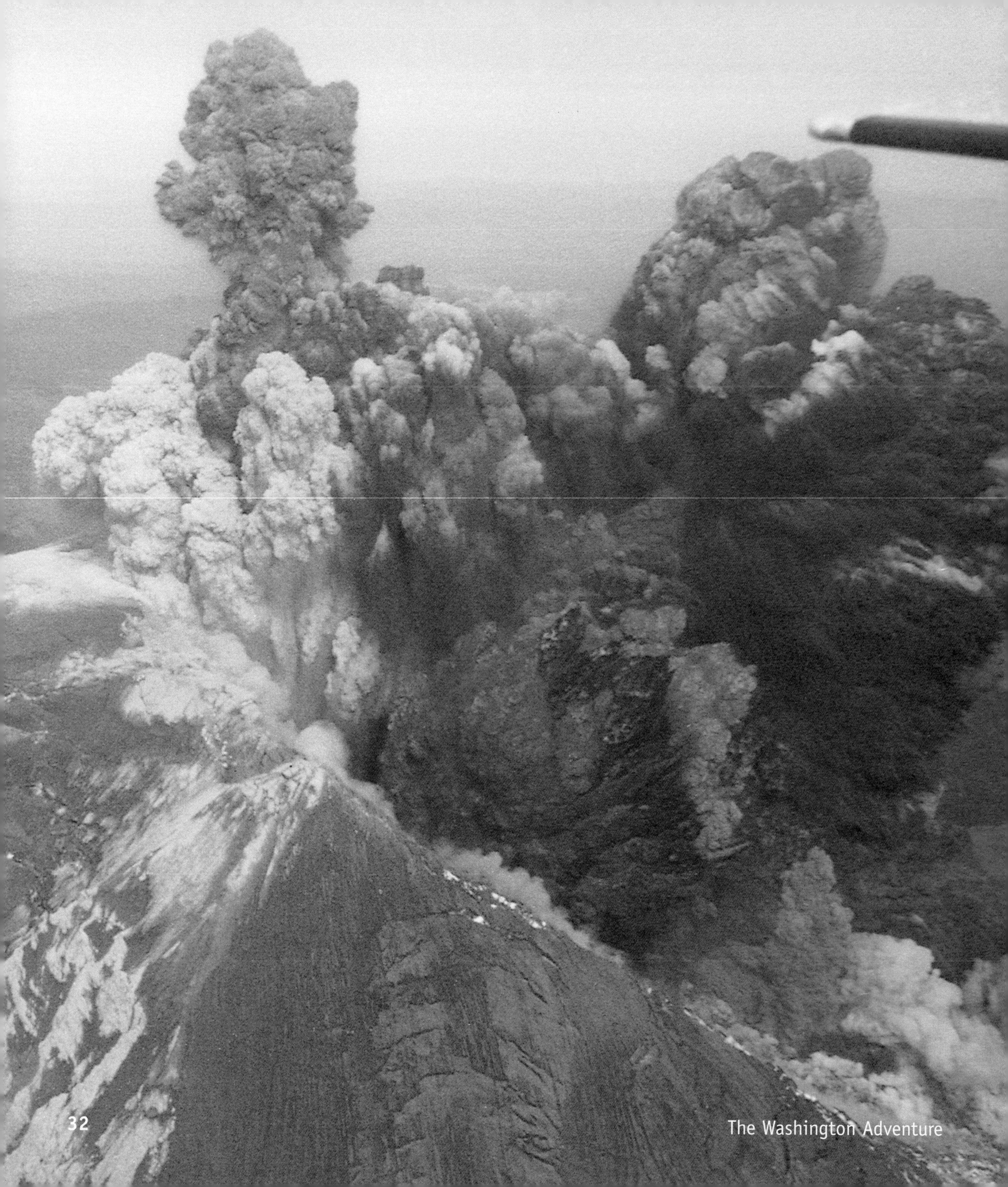

Mt. Saint Helens Erupts

Most changes in the earth happen slowly. Over many millions of years, mountains have been pushed up in Washington and then *eroded* away. These slow changes in the land still go on today.

Faster geological changes also take place here from time to time. The *eruption* of Mt. Saint Helens is one of them.

In early 1980, there were signs of danger. Some small earthquakes shook the land. Towers of steam rose from the mountain top. Scientists could tell that the mountain was swelling. Everyone was told to leave the area. Most people did. Still, no one knew exactly what might happen, or when.

On May 18, they found out! There was a huge explosion. Its force broke rocks into fine gray dust called ash. A fountain of ash shot nine miles into the sky. Winds blew the ash across the state. The ash filled the sky and blocked the sun. In the middle of the day, some parts of Washington were dark as night.

Highways, schools, and businesses were closed. People had to stay indoors. Meanwhile, snow on the mountain melted and mixed with dirt. Great rivers of mud filled up rivers, carrying away houses and causing huge floods.

It took months to clean up the ash and mud. It is taking much longer for the mountain environment to recover. If you visit Mt. Saint Helens today, you will see whole forests that were knocked down by the blast. You will also see plants that have grown back. Scientists are studying how the plants and animals come back after the eruption.

Other Volcanoes

Washington has five large volcanoes. They are sometimes called "sleeping giants" because they have erupted before and may erupt again. They are Mt. Rainier, Mt. Baker, Mt. Adams, and Glacier Peak. Mt. Rainier is near many large cities. If it erupts, it may cause mud flows that could go as far as Tacoma.

- Mt. Baker
- Glacier Peak

Mt. Rainer
•

Mt. Adams
•

Mt. St. Helens

This is how Mt. Saint Helens looks today. There is only a large crater where the top of the mountain used to be. Great rivers of mud and rocks and blasts of hot gas killed plants and animals.

Natural Washington

Mountains have been pushed up by moving plates of the earth's land masses and then worn away by erosion several times in Washington's past. Scientists say the Cascade Range is about 40 million years old.

The Washington Adventure

After the earthquake of 2001, a river of mud almost buried this home near Seattle.

PLATES ON THE MOVE

The surface of the earth is divided into large pieces called plates. These plates are moving slowly, all around the earth. These plate movements made Washington grow in the past. They pushed up the Cascade Mountains. The plates are still moving. That's why we have active volcanoes and earthquakes in Washington today.

Most earthquakes happen near the edges of plates. Washington is located at one of these places. There was a big earthquake in 2001, and there have been many other earthquakes in the past.

Earthquakes can damage buildings and freeways. They can shake heavy things off tables and walls.

It's important to be prepared for these events. Do you have an earthquake plan at home and at school?

Lesson 5

Memory Master

1. What do geologists study?
2. How were the rocks that cover much of eastern Washington formed?
3. What were the Ice Ages?
4. Tell two ways that Ice Age glaciers changed the land of our state.
5. Give two examples of geologic changes that are still going on today.

Chapter 1 Review

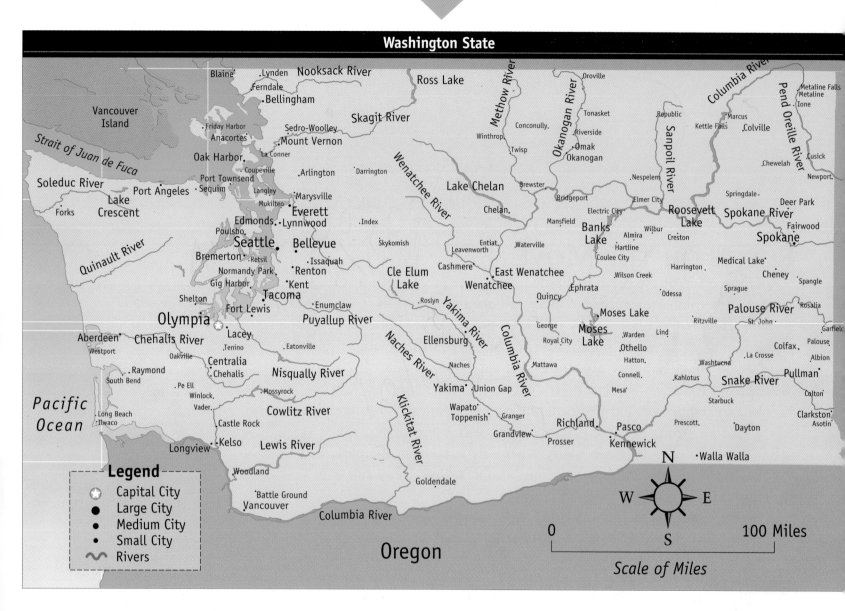

Washington State

(Map of Washington State showing cities, rivers, and lakes)

Blaine · Lynden · Nooksack River · Ross Lake · Oroville · Columbia River · Metaline Falls · Metaline · Ione

Ferndale · Bellingham · Methow River · Okanogan River · Tonasket · Pend Oreille River

Vancouver Island · Skagit River · Conconully · Republic · Kettle Falls · Marcus · Colville · Cusick

Strait of Juan de Fuca · Friday Harbor · Anacortes · Sedro-Woolley · Winthrop · Riverside · Omak · Okanogan · Nespelem · Chewelah · Newport

Soleduc River · Port Angeles · Oak Harbor · Coupeville · La Conner · Mount Vernon · Twisp · Lake Chelan · Brewster · Elmer City · Springdale · Deer Park

Lake Crescent · Forks · Port Townsend · Sequim · Arlington · Darrington · Wenatchee River · Chelan · Bridgeport · Electric City · Roosevelt Lake · Spokane River · Fairwood

Quinault River · Langley · Mukilteo · Marysville · Everett · Index · Skykomish · Mansfield · Banks Lake · Almira · Wilbur · Creston · Medical Lake · Spokane

Edmonds · Lynnwood · Leavenworth · Entiat · Waterville · Coulee City · Hartline · Harrington · Cheney · Spangle

Poulsbo · Seattle · Bellevue · Cashmere · East Wenatchee · Wilson Creek · Odessa · Sprague · Palouse River · Rosalia

Bremerton · Retsil · Issaquah · Cle Elum Lake · Roslyn · Wenatchee · Quincy · Ephrata · Moses Lake · Ritzville · St. John · Garfield

Normandy Park · Renton · Kent · Yakima River · George · Moses Lake · Warden · Lind · Colfax · Palouse

Gig Harbor · Shelton · Tacoma · Enumclaw · Naches River · Ellensburg · Columbia River · Royal City · Othello · Hatton · Washtucna · La Crosse · Albion

Fort Lewis · Puyallup River · Naches · Mattawa · Connell · Kahlotus · Snake River · Pullman

Olympia · Lacey · Eatonville · Yakima · Union Gap · Mesa · Starbuck · Colton

Aberdeen · Chehalis River · Tenino · Nisqually River · Wapato · Toppenish · Granger · Richland · Prescott · Dayton · Clarkston · Asotin

Westport · Oakville · Centralia · Chehalis · Grandview · Prosser · Pasco · Kennewick

Raymond · South Bend · Pe Ell · Winlock · Vader · Mossyrock · Cowlitz River · Klickitat River

Pacific Ocean · Long Beach · Ilwaco · Castle Rock · Lewis River · Walla Walla

Longview · Kelso · Woodland · Goldendale

Battle Ground · Vancouver · Columbia River

Oregon

Legend
- ★ Capital City
- ● Large City
- ● Medium City
- · Small City
- ~ Rivers

N · W · E · S

0   100 Miles

Scale of Miles

Activity

Where Do You Live?

Study this map and find where you live. Then answer these questions:

Do you live in one of these towns or cities? Which cities are closest to you? Which cities are the farthest away from you? Are there any rivers near you? How many miles are you from the ocean?

Activity

Reading a Map

There are many kinds of maps. Can you think of some? Perhaps you first thought of a road map. You might use it on a vacation. Your class has maps of the world and the United States. You could draw a map to get from the school to your home. Making a treasure map might be fun.

Maps help us get where we want to go. They help us understand where places are.

It is important to know how to read a map. Most maps have symbols you need to know about. Here are some of them:

Legend
- ✪ Capital City
- ● Large City
- ● Medium City
- • Small City
- 〜 Rivers

0   50 Miles

Scale of Miles

Compass: Maps show the directions north, south, east, and west. You'll find these directions on a compass symbol. Most maps have north at the top. It helps to read a map if you put the map so that you and the map are facing north. Then west will be on your left and east will be on your right. Where will south be?

Legend or Key: Mapmakers use symbols to stand for certain things such as cities, rivers, freeways, campgrounds, and airports. Whenever there are symbols, there is a **key** or **legend** that explains what the symbols mean. What do the symbols on this legend represent?

Scale of Miles: To show us distances, or how far apart places really are, mapmakers use a **scale of miles.** One inch on a map might mean 100 miles on the real land. Or one inch might stand for 1,000 miles, or even more. Look at this map and see how many miles are shown by one inch on the scale of miles. Look at a globe and see how many miles one inch stands for.

Activity

Natural and Political Boundaries

When the government divided our country into states, it used imaginary lines as boundaries. These are the **political boundaries** that you see on maps. People decided where the boundaries should be. They are not actually written on the earth.

Landforms such as mountains, rivers, and oceans form **natural boundaries.** The Columbia and Snake Rivers form part of our boundaries with Oregon and Idaho. It is easy for everyone to see and understand these boundaries.

1. What rivers form part of our boundaries?

2. What ocean is one of our natural boundaries?

3. What states touch our boundaries?

4. What country touches our boundary?

chapter 2

THE TIME
12,000 years ago–**1800s**

"In the old days . . . we relied on the baskets, the rivers, the lands, the roots, the berries, the fish, and the animals. Today, we live the [modern] life, but our hearts still travel where our ancestors lived and died."

—Liichaat Chehalis, from
A Time of Tribal Gathering: An
Intertribal Welcome

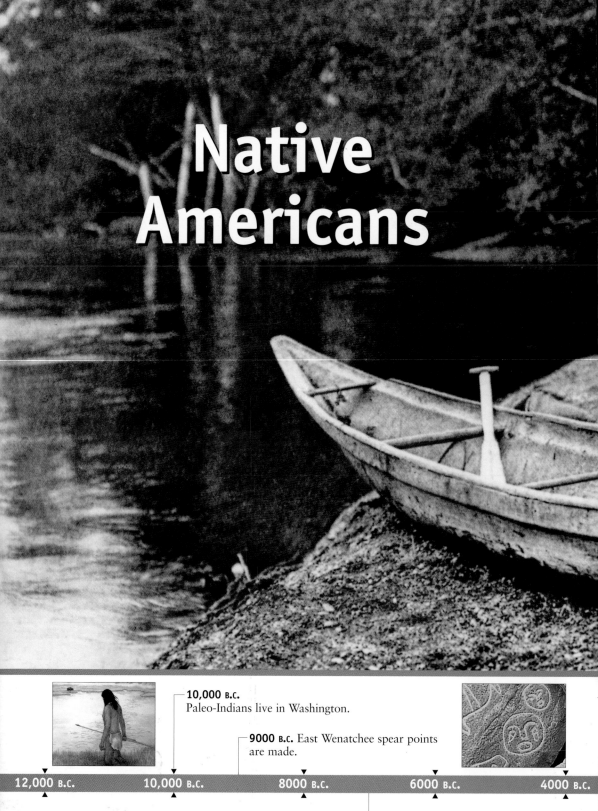

Native Americans

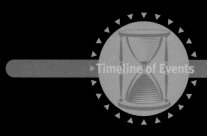

Timeline of Events

10,000 B.C.
Paleo-Indians live in Washington.

9000 B.C. East Wenatchee spear points are made.

| 12,000 B.C. | 10,000 B.C. | 8000 B.C. | 6000 B.C. | 4000 B.C. |

7000 B.C.
Kennewick Man lives near the Columbia River.

3000 B.C.
Cedar forests grow back after the Ice Ages.

Dates are about when scientists think these things happened.

One of Washington's most famous photographers, Edward Curtis, took this picture of an Indian fishing camp about 100 years ago. The house is made of tule. Tule is a plant that grows wild in Washington.

1500
A mudslide covers part of the village at Ozette.

1800s
First Europeans settle in Washington.

2000 B.C.	A.D. 1500	A.D. 1600	A.D. 1700	A.D. 1800

1500 B.C.
Coastal people begin to hunt seals and whales.

39

People made spears that had a spear point tied onto a stick. Later, people invented a tool called an **atlatl**. A hunter could throw a spear harder and faster with the atlatl.

Lesson 1

The First People

PEOPLE TO KNOW
Paleo-Indians

PLACES TO LOCATE
North America

WORDS TO UNDERSTAND
ancient
archaeologist
artifact
atlatl
extinct
petroglyph

Kennewick

WHO WERE THE FIRST PEOPLE?

The very first people in the place we call Washington probably came here at the end of the last Ice Age. Scientists call them Paleo-Indians. Native Americans call them the Ancient Ones.

We don't know much about these men, women, and children. They left no written records of their lives. However, they did leave clues about how they lived. They left spear points and other tools made from stone and bone. They left shells and bones from the food they ate and ashes from their cooking fires.

A Rare Find

Stone points made by Paleo-Indians have been found in many places across North America. But very few *ancient* human bones have ever been found. Bones can be very important. Scientists can study bones to learn what Paleo-Indians looked like.

In 1996, a human skeleton was discovered near Kennewick. It was buried along the shore of the Columbia River. This rare find became known as "Kennewick Man." It is about 9,000 years old. That makes it one of the oldest skeletons in North America.

The Washington Adventure

Archaeologists

Archaeologists are scientists who study clues to learn how people lived in the past. Many of these clues are *artifacts* buried in the earth. An artifact is something made by people.

How do archaeologists work? First, they mark off the site they will study. They want to know just where an object was found. This might give them clues about how an object was used.

Carefully, archaeologists remove one layer of dirt at a time. They keep careful notes about what they find. Even the smallest item may have a story to tell. It might give clues to what the people ate and what tools they made.

Stone spear points are among the oldest artifacts found in Washington. They are about 12,000 years old.

Spear points are some of the oldest artifacts. They are made of stone and last a long time.

Archaeologists keep careful records as they dig. They start by using string to mark off sections of the ground. They give each section a number. They also number each thing they find so they will know where it came from.

Activity

Artifacts

Artifacts are things made by people. Even today, people make things that might be studied by archaeologists in the future. Can you tell which of these things are artifacts and which are not?

- an arrow point
- a comic book
- a tree
- an ancient trash pile
- stones that were shaped into tools by people
- a river
- a piece of pottery

ANCIENT ANIMALS

At the end of the Ice Age, the land looked different than it does today. The climate was warming up and the glaciers were melting. The glaciers had scraped all the plants and soil away as they moved across the land. It took thousands of years for forests to cover the land again.

The animals that lived then were very different from the ones today. There were huge mammoths and mastodons. They looked something like very large elephants. There were large wildcats as big as lions and tiny horses as small as dogs. All these animals are now *extinct*. They no longer live anywhere on the earth.

Skilled Hunters and Stoneworkers

The first people may have come here following the wild animals. The people were skilled hunters. They killed large and small animals for food.

The people made spear points by chipping away at hard rock with sharp tools they had made from stones. The large stone points are some of the most beautiful and unusual artifacts found in Washington. Many were found in East Wenatchee.

The people left carvings in rock.

The people also made rock tools to carve designs into rock. Rock carvings are called *petroglyphs*. Many examples of ancient rock art have been found in Washington.

Paleo-Indian men hunted the huge mammoths and mastodons. They used the meat for food. They used the bones and tusks. What do you think they made from the bones?

Memory Master

Lesson 1

1. What do scientists call the first people who lived in Washington?

2. What do archaeologists do to help us learn about people who lived in the past?

3. Name some animals that lived at the end of the Ice Age.

4. List some artifacts from the Paleo-Indians.

The Washington Adventure

WHAT'S IN A NAME?

When Christopher Columbus arrived in America, he thought he was near India. He called the people who lived here "Indians." It soon became clear that Columbus had made a mistake, but the name stuck.

Today, several different words are used for the first people here, including Indian, American Indian, or Native American. *Native* means born in a place, or being naturally from a certain region. So we say there are native groups of people in a place. We also talk about native plants or animals. Other people, plants, or animals came later.

A long time ago, there were over forty groups, or tribes, of native people in Washington. They each had their own name for themselves in their own language. For example, *Duwamish* means "people living on the river." *Spokane* means "people of the sun."

TWO CULTURES

As the land and climate changed after the Ice Age, so did the people's ways of living. The way a group of people live is their *culture.* A cultural region is a place where people of the same culture live. Two Native American cultures became important in Washington. They are known as Coastal and Plateau.

Coastal people lived in villages west of the Cascade Mountains. Their villages were near the Pacific Ocean, Puget Sound, and other coastal waters. Plateau people lived east of the Cascades.

Each tribe was **unique** in some ways. But the tribes in each region also had much in common. They shared the same culture.

Most of today's Native Americans are the **descendants** of the people who lived here long ago. Are you?

The Coastal People

PEOPLE TO KNOW
Coastal people

PLACES TO LOCATE
India
Alaska
Oregon
Ozette
Pacific Coast
Cascade Mountains

WORDS TO UNDERSTAND
ceremony
controversial
culture
descendant
generous
harpoon
inherit
legend
native
potlatch
totem pole
unique
weir

Coastal Region

Plateau Region

Plains Region

If you lived in this plank house, your parents, brothers and sisters, aunts and uncles, and cousins might all live with you. A hole in the center of the roof would let out the smoke from cooking fires. What do you think the children whispered to each other at night?

Activity

Then and Now

Compare your own life to that of Indian children in the past. List three ways that your life is different from theirs and three ways it is the same.

Would you like to live the way they did? Write a sentence telling how you feel about this.

Coastal People

As you learned in Chapter 1, the land between the Pacific Ocean and the Cascade Mountains has a wet, mild climate. It is a perfect place for thick evergreen forests. In fact, forests once covered most of the western half of our state. Traveling through forests wasn't easy, so Coastal people spent most of their lives near the sea. They used canoes to travel from place to place. The sea was also a rich source of food all year long.

Coastal Villages

Have you ever wanted to travel back in time? Pretend for a moment that you can go back hundreds of years. Imagine standing on a beach along Puget Sound. This is a village where Coastal people live. There were once many villages like this along the Pacific Northwest Coast.

Along the beach is a row of wooden houses. They are made of large wooden planks held up by poles. Behind the houses is a thick forest. A stream of cold clean water runs through the forest and down to the sandy beach. Many carved wooden canoes have been pulled up along the sand.

The Washington Adventure

People are everywhere. Fathers and mothers are working and talking. Children are playing along the shore or splashing in the water. When more canoes come into sight, the children wave to welcome them.

Inside the wooden houses are rows of wide wooden shelves along the walls. These are places where the families sleep and store things. In the center of the house, a fire burns in a ring of stones. The fires are important for light and cooking. Fires also keep people warm. A visitor might see and smell dried salmon hanging from the ceiling.

Childhood on the Coast

Imagine that you live in the village. What would your life be like?

Coastal villages had no schools. Children learned by watching and listening and by helping adults. Boys helped hunt and fish. They learned to make and use fishing tools. Girls helped gather and prepare food. Taking care of babies and helping to make clothes was also the work of the girls.

Most of the time, the people didn't wear many clothes. When it rained, however, they wore hats and capes. When it was very cold, they wore warm robes.

Food was always easy to find along the beach. Children helped gather clams, mussels, oysters, and crabs when the tide went out. Even today, you may hear Coastal people say, "When the tide is out, the table is set." What does this saying mean?

It was easy to find food. Children gathered shellfish on the beaches.

Weavers wove yarn to make warm robes. To make the yarn, they spun plant fibers, animal hair, and wool together. They even wove in the hair from a special kind of dog. Rain cloaks were woven from cedar bark and mountain goat fur.

Hundreds of salmon are drying at a fishing camp. The dried fish were eaten all year.

A man spears a fish at a weir. This photo was taken about 100 years ago.

Salmon

Salmon were an important food.

The most important food was salmon. It is hard now to imagine how many salmon swam up the rivers each year. In a few weeks, people could catch enough fish to last the whole year.

The return of the salmon each spring was an important event. When the first salmon of the year was caught, there was a **ceremony.** All the people in the village thanked the salmon for giving them food. Then the fishing season began.

Native Americans knew many ways to catch salmon. One way was to build a wooden fence, or *weir,* across a stream. The salmon could not swim past it. With a spear or net, a fisherman could pull out one fish after another.

Some of the fish were eaten fresh. The rest had to be dried and stored for later. The women cut each fish, cleaned it, and removed the bones. Then they hung the fish on wooden racks over smoky fires. Smoking and drying the fish kept them from spoiling. They would last until the next salmon-fishing season.

The people dried other foods, too. They spread berries in the sun. They made cakes from wild roots and dried them. Of course, dried foods are not as tasty as fresh foods, so children dipped their food in fish oil before eating it.

Grandmother Cedar

Just as important as salmon to Coastal people was the cedar tree. Western red cedar is special in several ways. Its wood lasts a long time, even in a rainy climate. It can also be split fairly easily into long, straight boards.

Coastal tribes used huge cedar planks to make their houses. They used smaller boards to make cradles, beds, and storage boxes. They carved cedar logs into canoes.

The bark of the cedar is also special. Its inner layer is soft and stringy. Coastal people used it to weave baskets, mats, hats, and clothing. They twisted strings of bark together to make strong ropes. They even pounded and softened bark to use for baby diapers.

Cedar planks were used to make houses.

WHAT IS A POTLATCH?

Today, our government keeps written records of births, weddings, and other important events. Coastal people did not write words. However, they had a way to share and remember these things. It was a special ceremony called a *potlatch*.

Suppose you are a chief. You have just **inherited** important family treasures, and you want everyone to know this. You ask members of your family to help you plan a potlatch. Together, you begin gathering food and gifts. This might take months or even years.

Finally, you are ready to invite guests. You send canoes out to other villages to tell people about the potlatch. When the guests arrive, they are dressed in their fine clothes. They are welcomed to the village with chants and dances.

Then comes the potlatch. You and your family wear special robes. You perform your songs and dances. You display the family treasures. Then you give each of your guests a gift and invite them to eat at a big feast. By accepting the gifts, each guest promises to remember the event. In this way, guests keep records for the tribe.

A modern-day potlatch still has gifts, a feast, songs, and dances.

▶ Photo by Brian Wallace

Learning from Legends

Children learned about their world by listening to **legends**. Legends are stories that tell about the past. Through legends, children learned important lessons. They learned to treat all living things with respect. They learned to think of the earth as the **generous** mother shared by all creatures. Imagine sitting with your family around you on a dark winter night, listening to this story.

The Girl Who Lived at Lake Crescent

There once was a girl who lived at Lake Crescent with her stepmother. Everybody in the house used to help with the work, but not this girl. She would lie down by the fire and sleep and sleep. Her dress was dirty. Her hair was tangled.

Her stepmother was tired of this. She said, "Still asleep? *Whik bakah, Whik bakah*. Lazy bones!" The girl was upset because all the other girls had pretty names. She walked to the lake and began to cry. She cried and cried. The waterfalls around Lake Crescent are her tears.

She heard a voice say, "Why are you crying?" The girl looked around and saw a flock of white swans. She answered, "Nobody loves me. They say I don't know how to do anything. My stepmother calls me *Whik bakah*."

"Why don't you stay with us?" asked the swans. "We will tell you all we know." The leader of the swans told the girl to get on his back and close her eyes. She climbed on and could feel herself going way up. When she opened her eyes, she was on the top of the Olympic Mountains.

The swans showed her how to take cedar bark from a tree. They showed her how to weave it and make a dress trimmed with duck feathers in pretty colors. They showed her how to make baskets of cedar bark and bear grass, and baskets of spruce root to carry wood. She learned what was good to eat in the woods. She was gone so long that her stepmother thought she had died.

The white swan said, "Now that you know all you need to know, you are ready to go home. You may take all the things you made." The girl climbed on the swan's back and was soon home. She thanked the swans.

Her stepmother didn't recognize her at first! Then she gave her a big hug. She gave a potlatch and gave the girl a good name. The girl gave each of the guests a present of something she had made herself. She was happy.

—told by Helen Peterson, Makah, published in *The History and Culture of the Indians of Washington State: A Curriculum Guide*

COASTAL ART

The Coastal people are famous for wood carving and weaving. Boys learned carving skills and girls learned weaving. The people also carved designs into rock.

Artists were very important people. A good canoe carver was respected and wealthy. A woman who wove fine clothes or baskets was also rewarded.

Totem poles are the most famous examples of Coastal art, but they were not made in Washington. The tribes that made totem poles in the old days lived farther north, in Canada and Alaska. Those tribes used totem poles as a way to display their family histories.

Each figure on the wooden pole told a story. The family treasured each story. This was true of many works of Coastal art, including animal designs and even songs and dances. No one else could use them. A wealthy family might own many dances, many beautiful carvings, and many fine baskets.

Makah mask

Totem poles told a family history. Coastal people in Alaska made this one.

▲ Mask photo by Richard Cummins

Native American artists carried on the traditions of Pacific Northwest tribes. This man carved canoes as an art form. He even carved people to sit inside the canoe.

The Washington Adventure

Whales provided food and oil for the Makah.

WHALE HUNTERS OF THE COAST

All Washington tribes had hunting skills. The Makah, however, were one of the few tribes who hunted whales. This was a dangerous job.

Whale hunters prepared carefully, taking time to rest and pray. Finally, the time of the hunt arrived. The hunters paddled out to sea in large, beautifully carved canoes. When they spotted a whale, the hunt began.

There was no room for mistakes. One canoe came up close to the animal's left side. The chief hunter thrust his *harpoon* into the whale's huge body. The whale jerked wildly. This canoe had to move away quickly!

A second canoe came up from the other side. Another man thrust a harpoon into the whale. Long ropes and floats had been attached to the harpoons. The floats were seal skins filled with air. These made it hard for the animal to swim and dive. Now the whale was dragging two long ropes and many floats.

When the whale finally got tired, the canoes came in closer. The hunters killed the whale with more harpoons and pulled it to shore.

Everyone in the village came to meet the canoes. They gave thanks for a safe hunt. Whale meat and oil were favorite foods. Everyone shared in the feast.

Modern Whale Hunts

As modern towns and cities grew in Washington, the American Indians did things differently than they had before. The Makah tribe stopped hunting whales. Some people began to think this was not good. "Whale hunting is an important part of our tradition," they said. "It is a way to feel proud about who we are."

In the 1990s, the tribe asked for a special permit to hunt a gray whale. In the past, big whaling businesses had killed thousands of whales. Some kinds of whales had almost become extinct. Countries around the world had agreed to stop hunting in order to protect the whales.

By 1990, however, there were lots of gray whales again. Still, many people did not want the Makahs to kill even one of them.

The Makahs finally got a permit and went ahead with their hunt. Other people tried to stop them, but in 1999, they killed one whale. The whale meat was shared by tribal members and potlatch guests.

Two Makah Indian whalers stand on top of a dead gray whale in 1999.

The Ozette Dig

One of the most exciting discoveries in Washington took place in the 1970s. The old Native American village of Ozette was discovered on the coast. The people who had lived there were members of the Makah tribe. The men hunted whales.

About 500 years ago, a great mudslide buried their village. Whole houses were buried. The mud kept out air and stopped things from rotting. It was a good place to study artifacts.

Archaeologists and modern Makah people worked together to uncover the village and study what they found. There were more than 50,000 artifacts. They included tools, baskets, and other objects of everyday life.

This carving of an orca fin is the most famous artifact found at Ozette. It is decorated with sea otter teeth. You can see it at the Makah museum in Neah Bay.

What do you think?

The modern whale hunt was ***controversial.*** Hunting whales was part of the Makah culture, but the people no longer needed whales for food. Do you think the Makah should hunt whales today? Why or why not?

Activity

Let's Play!
Indian children learned a lot about the plants and animals around them. One way to learn and remember was through games. Here are two games you can try.

Crab Race:
Players stand behind the starting line, facing sideways. When they hear "Go!" they drop to their hands and knees and race sideways to the finish line.

Bear Race:
Mark a starting line and a finish line. Racers must stand behind the starting line until they hear the word "Go!" Then they place their hands on the ground and head forward, moving the right hand and right foot forward at the same time and then the left hand and left foot. The first one to cross the finish line by moving only in this way is the winner.

Lesson 2

Memory Master

1. Columbus called the people Indians because he thought he was near _____.
2. What kind of houses did Coastal people live in?
3. What kinds of work did Coastal children do?
4. The most important food was _____.
5. How did the people use wood from the cedar tree?
6. During a potlatch, what did a family give to their guests?
7. Stories told about the past are called_____.

Tall tule rushes were cut, dried, and laid flat side by side. The ends were tied to form mats. Tule mats were laced to a log framework and overlapped to provide more protection from wind and rain.

Lesson 3

Plateau People

PEOPLE TO KNOW
Plateau people
Plains Indians

PLACES TO LOCATE
Rocky Mountains
Columbia Plateau
Columbia River
Great Plains

WORDS TO UNDERSTAND
button blanket
family crest
powwow
respect
shaman
teepee
tule

LIFE ON THE COLUMBIA PLATEAU

East of the Cascades, the dry climate was very different from the wet land of the coast. Since the people of the plateau did not have many trees to build wooden houses and since they could not eat seafoods from the ocean, they had a different culture.

Imagine that you are traveling back in time once again. Imagine yourself on the plateau. You see families living in large, snug longhouses all winter long. The longhouses are made from wood poles, covered with *tule* mats. These thick, woven mats made warm walls. They were also used to sit and sleep on.

Peek inside a longhouse. A fire in the center keeps the children warm. Families sit around it, working, talking, and laughing.

Salmon Fishing

Now it is springtime. The snow is gone, and the air is growing warmer. The hills and valleys that stretch out around you are green with new plants. For the children, this is an exciting time of year. It is time for salmon fishing. It's time to travel to the fishing camps.

Camas

One of the most important native foods was the root of the camas plant. The camas lily has a lovely flower and a tasty root. The root is a round bulb. The bulbs look like small round onions and taste something like sweet potatoes.

Women gathered the camas bulbs in small baskets like this one.

Native women covered each layer of bulbs with moss in large fire pits and left them to dry. The families ate camas whole or added chopped camas to fish and meat.

Each group has its own fishing spot. Many are along the Columbia River.

Salmon fishing days are a time for both work and play. There are horse races, foot races, and games. There is time for visiting and trading with other tribes of the coast and plateau.

Hunting and Gathering Seasons

When summer came to the plateau, it was time to move again. The women and girls went out to gather berries and nuts and dig wild roots. Men and boys went hunting. On the plateau as on the coast, children learned about their culture by helping adults.

The main hunting season came in early fall. Hunters made arrows from wood and attached sharp stone points. They made bows from wood or the horns of mountain sheep. They made spears, traps, and other hunting tools. They hunted deer, rabbits, mountain goats, sheep, and birds.

From the skins of the animals, women made warm leather clothing. In the old days, they decorated the clothing with feathers, shells, and porcupine quills. Later, they used colored beads.

Plateau women are famous for their beautiful weaving and beadwork.

PLATEAU LEADERS

In Plateau tribes, there was little difference between rich and poor. A group of wise and *respected* adults made the rules and decided what should be done. Leaders with different skills had different duties. For example, a brave and skilled fighter might lead the tribe in war.

Older people were treated with great respect.

> I [saw] an old woman in one of the lodges. . . . She was blind . . . and had lived more than 100 winters. She [had] the best place in the house, and when she spoke, great attention was paid to what she said.
>
> —from the journals of Lewis and Clark

Older people are still repected by Coastal and Plateau people. They are called elders. Many are important leaders. Vi Hilbert is one of them. She is a teacher of native language and legends.

Shamans

One kind of leader in both Coastal and Plateau tribes was the *shaman.* Shamans were spiritual leaders who also had the job of healing the sick.

Native Americans believed that all things, including plants, rocks, and animals, had spirits. They believed these spirits could sometimes cause diseases. When a person was sick, both the body and the spirit needed to be healed.

Shamans were men or women with special power over spirits. They used medicines made from plants to help heal people. They also used special spiritual songs and dances.

HORSES COME TO THE PLATEAU

Coastal villages had plenty of seafood nearby to eat all year, but Plateau people had to travel to find food. Horses made this travel much easier.

Long ago, before the Ice Ages, early kinds of horses lived in North America. However, those small horses became extinct. The first horses of the kind we know today were brought to America about 500 years ago by the Spanish explorers.

Native Americans soon learned how useful horses could be. People on horseback could travel farther in search of food. Horses could carry heavy loads. Hunters on horses could find and hunt large animals such as buffalo and deer.

Plateau people first got horses by trading with tribes from the Great Plains. Some of the Plateau tribes, such as the Palouse and the Nez Perce, had thousands of beautiful horses. The people were very skilled at raising and riding them.

The famous Appaloosa horses were named for the Palouse tribe that raised them.

A girl sits on a horse at the famous Pendleton Round-Up in Oregon. Which things in the photo come from the Plains Indians?

Great Plains

Buffalo Hunters of the Great Plains

The best known Native American cultures are those of the Great Plains. The Great Plains are vast, grassy lands east of the Rocky Mountains. They were the home of the buffalo. The Plains Indians were skilled horsemen and buffalo hunters. They ate buffalo meat and made **teepees** out of buffalo skins. They wore leather leggings, shirts, and moccasins.

Plateau people learned to make teepees from their neighbors on the Great Plains. They strapped the tall thin teepee poles to horses that pulled them like sleds. This was a good way to move their belongings from place to place.

The Plains Indians are the Indians most often seen in movies, but they are just one of the many native cultures of North America.

The Washington Adventure

In Spokane, modern American Indians hold a powwow. They dress in native clothes, dance, and eat. The celebration lasts for several days.

NATIVE AMERICANS TODAY

Until about 200 years ago, all of Washington was Indian land. Native Americans were the only people who lived here.

Today, Native Americans make up just a small part of Washington's population. Potlatches, *powwows,* and other traditions are still important, but Native Americans now live in towns and go to jobs or schools with other people in our state. The Native American way of life has changed.

In this book, you will read about those changes. You will learn about other groups of people who came to Washington and how the lives of Native Americans changed as a result.

Lesson
3

Memory Master

1. Did the Plateau people live in a wet or dry climate?
2. What kind of winter house did the early Plateau people make?
3. What important native food did the people eat?
4. What kinds of work did children do?
5. What did shamans do to help the people?
6. What large animals were hunted by the Indians of the Great Plains?

Native Americans

Chapter 2 Review

Activity

Many places in Washington and Idaho are named for the tribes that used to live in the area. Read this list of tribal names. Which are now the names of places near you? Use a map to help you find these places.

Some Coastal Tribes

Clallam	Quinault	Nooksack
Chinook	Chehalis	Puyallup
Hoh	Cowlitz	Samish
Klallam	Duwamish	Skagit
Makah	Lummi	Snoqualmie
Ozette	Muckleshoot	Suquamish
Queets	Nisqually	Willapa

Some Plateau Tribes

Cayuse	Klickitat	San Poil
Chelan	Kootenai	Spokane
Coeur d'Alene	Metho	Wallula
Columbia	Nespelem	Wanapam
Colville	Nez Perce	Wenatchee
Kalispel	Okanogan	Wishram
Kittitas	Palouse	Yakima

Activity

Design a Family Crest

Study the potlatch photo on page 47 and the photo at the right. Look at the **button blanket** that the woman is wearing. Designs are outlined with buttons. They show **family crests.** Each crest tells a story in the family's history.

To make your own family crest, first think of something brave or wonderful in your family history. It might be something your parents or grandparents did. It might be a custom your family shares. Draw a simple picture of it. This is your crest.

Now make a button blanket with your crest design. You will need two squares of cloth or paper, one that is red and one that is dark blue or black. (Felt squares work well for this.) Using chalk, trace your crest design on the red square. Cut it out and paste it on the dark square. Then outline your design with white dots. You can use white paint or stick-on dots from an office store. These take the place of buttons, which are used on real button blankets.

Remember, no one can use your family crest without your permission!

Geography Tie-In

What natural resources did Coastal and Plateau people use to meet their basic needs? List as many as you can.

Archaeologist for a Day

Pretend you are an archaeologist. You have studied two sites in Washington. These lists show the artifacts you found at each site.

From what you have learned about the Paleo-Indians, the Coastal people, and the Plateau people in this chapter, can you name the culture that lived at each site?

Artifacts at Site A (9,000 years old)

stone spear points

piece of mammoth bone

ashes from a fire

Artifacts at Site B (300 years old)

fish hook made of bone

clam shells

part of a wooden bowl

Two Cultures

Compare the cultures of the Coastal people and the Plateau people. On a separate piece of paper, make two lists, one for each group. Use these words to help you.

Geography	Coastal People	Plateau People
Where did they live?		
Climate of the region		
Vegetation of the region		
Culture		
Houses		
Food		
Transportation		

Technology

Technology means the tools, skills, and knowledge that people need to meet their basic needs.

- Give two examples of the tools, skills, and knowledge that Native Americans needed for fishing or hunting.
- Give two examples of the tools, skills, and knowledge your family uses to get food.
- Who had an easier time getting food, a Native American family of the past or your family today?

"The weather was cold, the gales of wind were strong, and sometimes violent. . . . We were short of water, and had an unknown coast to explore."

—John Ledyard, sailor with Captain Cook, 1778

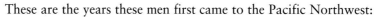

Timeline of Events

These are the years these men first came to the Pacific Northwest:

1542 Bartolome Ferrelo

1450	1500	1550	1600

1578 Sir Francis Drake

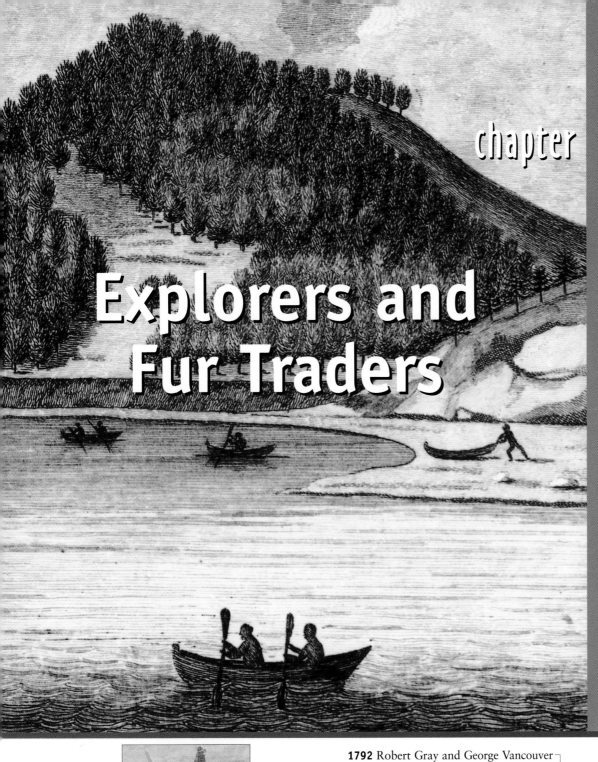

chapter 3

Explorers and Fur Traders

Native Americans paddle out to an explorer's ship in 1789. The Native Americans traded furs for metal tools, glass beads, and other things they wanted.

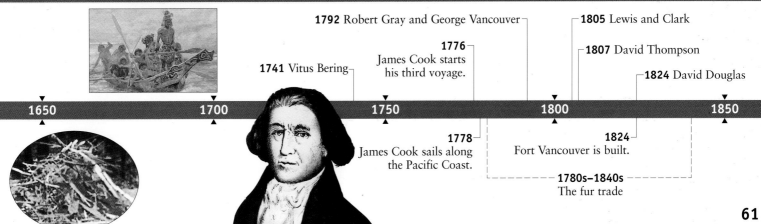

1792 Robert Gray and George Vancouver

1805 Lewis and Clark

1776 James Cook starts his third voyage.

1807 David Thompson

1741 Vitus Bering

1824 David Douglas

| 1650 | 1700 | 1750 | 1800 | 1850 |

1778 James Cook sails along the Pacific Coast.

1824 Fort Vancouver is built.

1780s–1840s The fur trade

VOYAGES TO UNKNOWN LANDS

Native Americans have lived here for thousands of years. For most of this time, they were the only people here. Other people in the world knew nothing about the Pacific Northwest. They did not even know it existed!

The first visitors to our region were *explorers.* They are people who go to new lands to learn about them. Each explorer hoped to find great riches. He might also find lands to claim for his country.

Ships from Spain, England, Russia, and other countries sailed along the coasts of North and South America. Each country hoped to be the first to find new lands, new treasures, and new routes for trade.

New Wonders from the New World

The journeys of the explorers caused great excitement in Europe. Their ships returned with many things that the people had never seen before. There were amazing birds and animals. There were new foods such as corn, beans, and potatoes. All of these things came from the land they called the "New World."

Spanish Ships Are the First to Arrive

The first explorer to see the Northwest was from Spain. Bartolome Ferrelo sailed up the Pacific coast from Mexico. Many years later, other Spanish explorers sailed the Washington coast. They named the San Juan Islands. They claimed all the land around the Strait of Juan de Fuca. Explorers helped Spain become the strongest country in the world.

Hispanic Ancestors

Many of the first explorers to North America sailed from Spain. They claimed much of the land in America, including today's Florida, many of the western states, and Mexico.

Spanish explorers, *missionaries,* and soldiers started churches, forts, farms, ranches, and towns. Some of these places grew into big cities.

Today, many **Hispanic** Americans have **ancestors** from these early settlements.

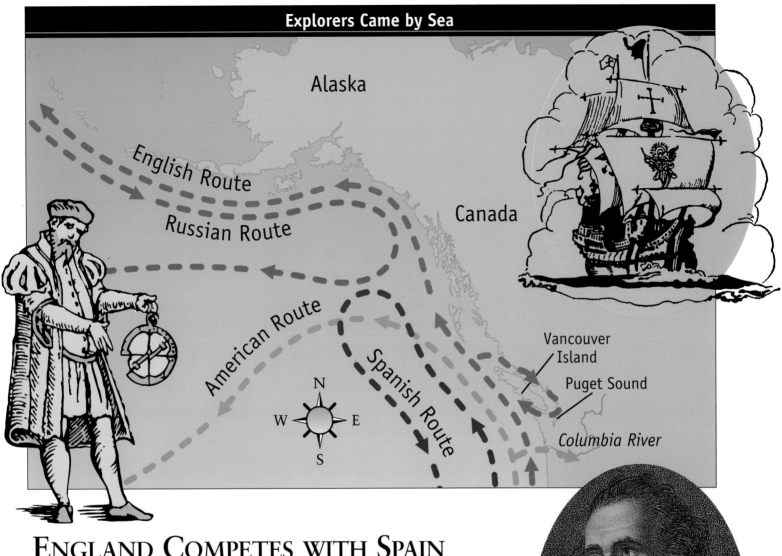

Alaska

English Route

Russian Route

Canada

American Route

Spanish Route

N
W   E
S

Vancouver
Island

Puget Sound

Columbia River

ENGLAND COMPETES WITH SPAIN

Other Europeans hoped to *challenge* Spain's power. One of them was Sir Francis Drake, a skilled English sea captain. Drake had seen Spanish ships carrying New World treasures home to Spain. He and his men decided they could attack and rob the Spanish ships and take their treasures home to England. He also helped explore new land for England. Some people believe he was the second explorer to see the Northwest coast.

What do you think?

Many English people believed that Drake was helping his country. They called him a *patriot.* Other people believed he was just a *pirate.* A pirate was someone who robbed ships. What do you think?

Captain Drake

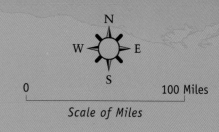

Russia

Bering Strait

Alaskan Frontier

0   100 Miles

Scale of Miles

Bering Sea

Gulf of Alaska

Aleutian Islands

Pacific Ocean

Hunting the Sea Otter

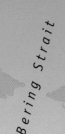

Sea otters are fun to watch, but they were not easy to hunt. This is how Native Americans hunted them:

Two skilled hunters sit in each of two very small canoes. They use bows and arrows and a small harpoon or spear. They go among the rocks in search of their prey. There is a fierce battle between the otter and the hunters, who are wounded by the claws and teeth of the animal.

WARM FURS FOR COLD LANDS

Gold was the treasure that Drake wanted the most. But the New World had many other *valuable* resources, too. Here in the Northwest, one natural resource became very important. Can you guess what it was?

The answer might surprise you. It's sea otter fur! You may have seen sea otters in a zoo. Today, otters are playful and fun to watch. They used to be valued for their soft warm fur.

Find the Aleutian Islands on the map. The native people there made clothing from sea otter furs. The furs kept them warm in the long winters.

The first European to stop in the islands was Vitus Bering. He made two important trips. On his first trip, he explored the water between Russia and Alaska. This body of water is now called the Bering Strait.

Then Bering sailed farther south along the coast of Alaska. On his way back, he stopped in the Aleutian Islands. He returned to Russia with his ship loaded with sea otter furs. The furs became very popular in the cold lands of Russia and China.

More Russian ships sailed along the Pacific coast. Along the way, they traded with native hunters for sea otter furs. In the years that followed, other explorers visited the Northwest coast. Fur trading became another reason to make the trip.

THE NORTHWEST PASSAGE

As more explorers came, they found other resources in the Northwest, too. They found fish and forests and animals that had thick warm fur. They found rich lands where people might settle.

However, there was one thing that the explorers never found—the Northwest Passage. They never found it because it does not exist!

For a very long time, Europeans thought there must be a way to sail from ocean to ocean all the way across North America. The country that found this route would have an easier way to sail between Europe and Asia. The control of this route would bring riches and power.

Many explorers tried to find a Northwest Passage. They searched all along the coasts. They sailed into bays and up rivers. But the rivers always came to an end. There was no way for ships to cross North or South America.

Captain Cook

Captain James Cook was one of the most important English explorers. Before coming to the Northwest, he had already sailed around the world twice. He had found the islands we now call Hawaii. He called them the Sandwich Islands.

Captain Cook came to the Pacific Coast to find the Northwest Passage. After sailing all the way up the coast, he decided that the passage did not exist.

However, Cook did learn about the Northwest. He wrote about the sea otters, fish, and great forests.

Activity

Writing in a Journal

The early explorers wrote in a journal, or diary, almost every day. That is how we know so much about them. They wrote about storms at sea. They wrote about getting sick or being lonely. They wrote how excited they were when they came close to land. They wrote about the places they saw and the people they met.

Keep a journal for a week or more. In a notebook, put the date first, then write what you did that day, who you saw, what you learned, and what you felt. A few years from now, you'll love reading your journal.

Lesson 1

Memory Master

1. What is an explorer?
2. What kinds of things did the explorers hope to find?
3. List three countries that sent explorers to the New World.
4. Why did explorers want to find a Northwest Passage?
5. What natural resources did Captain Cook write about?

More Explorers

PEOPLE TO KNOW
William Clark
David Douglas
Robert Gray
Meriwether Lewis
Alexander Mackenzie
Sacagawea
George Vancouver
York

PLACES TO LOCATE
Scotland
British Columbia
Vancouver Island
Oregon
Idaho
Massachusetts
St. Louis, Missouri
Astoria, Oregon
Rocky Mountains
San Juan Islands
Puget Sound
Nootka Sound
Columbia River
Missouri River

WORDS TO UNDERSTAND
botanist
interpreter

The waters at the entrance of the Columbia River were so rough that Robert Gray's crew saw whole trees being swept downstream.

AN AMERICAN EXPLORER

While explorers were sailing along the coast of the Pacific Northwest, a new country, the United States of America, was getting started on the other side of the continent.

News of the riches of the Northwest was exciting to Americans, too. A group of men in the United States had a bold plan. They loaded a ship with metal knives, beads, blankets, and other goods for trading. They hired Robert Gray to be the captain of the ship.

Gray and his crew sailed from Massachusetts all the way around South America. Then they sailed north, following the Pacific Coast. They got to what seemed to be a river, but the water was so rough the ships could not sail into it.

A month later, the crew again tried to sail into the river, but sandbars blocked the way. Gray waited until the ocean tides were high, then carefully guided a small boat, and then his ship, over the foamy white waves. This time he made it. He entered the Columbia River.

The crew spent ten days on the Columbia River, trading with the Indians for furs. Then the group sailed out to the ocean.

Gray sailed on to China and traded furs for Chinese silks, spices, and tea. Finally, his ship went around Asia and Africa and returned to the United States. There the Chinese goods were sold at high prices.

Gray's voyage was important in several ways:

- He was the first non-Indian explorer to sail up the mouth of the Columbia River.

- He started an important trading route to China.

- He was the first American to sail around the world.

Other traders followed Gray's route, and some became very rich. However, so many sea otters were killed that they almost became extinct. The sea otter trade ended.

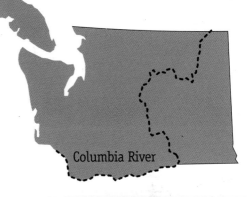

When Gray's ship arrived at Nootka on Vancouver Island, the men at the fort gave the sailors gifts of fresh vegetables. "I thought it a very handsome present."

—A crew member

Gray's Route from Boston to China

Robert Gray and his crew stopped at Nootka Sound on Vancouver Island. It became a center for Spanish and English fur traders.

Robert Gray

Explorers and Fur Traders

CLAIMING THE LAND

As explorers traveled, each claimed new lands for his country. Robert Gray claimed all the land along the Columbia River for the United States. That same year, an English captain named George Vancouver was the first non-Indian to explore Puget Sound. He made the first maps of the area and claimed all the lands around it for England.

For many years, the United States, England, and Spain all claimed the land we now call Washington.

George Vancouver explored and claimed the lands around Puget Sound. He named the Sound for Peter Puget, one of the men on his ship.

What do you think?

The land the explorers claimed for England, Spain, Russia, and the United States was already the home of Native American groups. Their ancestors had lived on the land for many years.

Do you think it was right or wrong for the explorers to think they could claim the land?

Danger!

Think of sailing in a small wooden ship to lands you know nothing about! If the winds are not strong enough, you might be stuck in a place for days. There might also be long weeks with terrible storms and no place to land. You might run out of food and fresh water.

You will have to sail all the way around South America.

The rocky coast kept explorers out to sea.

There are often big storms at the tip of South America. It is very cold. Some ships are lost at sea.

Once you get to the Northwest, waves crash into rocky cliffs. Heavy fog hides the land. Ships usually stay far from shore.

Try to imagine yourself in Captain Vancouver's ship as you read these notes from his journal:

Monday, 16 April, 1792

The surf broke with great violence. . . . The nearest shore was about 2 miles distant. . . . The rain and fog [kept us from] seeing much of this part of the coast.

Activity

Spanish captains named the San Juan Islands.

Naming the New Land

The explorers gave names to the places they saw.

- Spanish explorers named the San Juan Islands and the nearby waters.

- George Vancouver named Puget Sound, Mt. Rainier, Whidbey Island, and Hood Canal after men he knew.

- Robert Gray named the Columbia River after his ship.

Many places were later named for the explorers themselves. Look at a map of the Northwest to see how many places you can find that are named after the explorers.

EXPLORING BY LAND

The first explorers sailed along the coast. They rarely went ashore. Later, other explorers traveled along the rivers and across the land. They saw the mountains and river valleys and met the native people who lived there. They learned more about the land.

Alexander Mackenzie, a fur trader from Canada, was the first to cross the Northwest to the Pacific coast by land. He explored the rivers of British Columbia. One of them was named for him. Can you find it on a map?

WASHINGTON PORTRAIT

David Douglas
1799–1834

As a child in Scotland, David Douglas loved nature. He had to walk six miles to school each day and was often late. He spent too much time looking at the animals and plants he saw along the way. He was not a good student.

When he was eleven, David's father took him out of school and found him a job. It was the most wonderful job—helping in the gardens of a palace. David learned all he could. He read every book about plants he could find. In his spare time, he hiked around Scotland and studied wild plants.

As a young man, Douglas became a friend of the best-known *botanists* of his time. He dreamed of traveling and finding new plants that no one in Europe had seen before. He got his wish in 1824 when he sailed on a ship to the Pacific Northwest.

Douglas stayed for two years. He traveled with fur traders up the Columbia River and found almost 500 new kinds of plants. He became one of the most famous botanists of his time. The Douglas fir tree was named for him.

▼ Photo by Teresa Ogle

Lewis and Clark's Journey

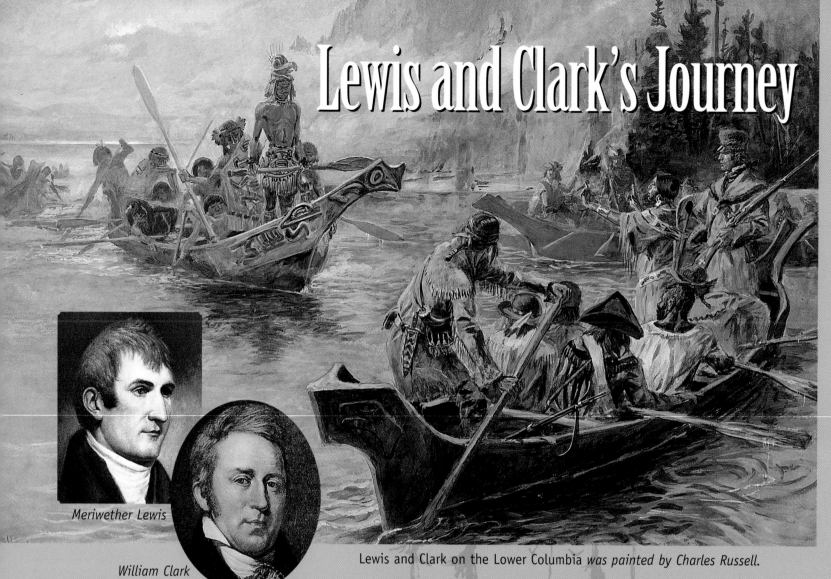

Meriwether Lewis

William Clark

Lewis and Clark on the Lower Columbia *was painted by Charles Russell.*

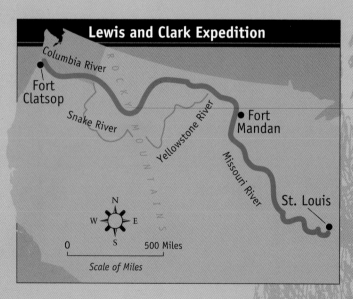

Lewis and Clark Expedition

Columbia River

Fort Clatsop

Snake River

Yellowstone River

Fort Mandan

Missouri River

St. Louis

ROCKY MOUNTAINS

N
W — E
S

0   500 Miles

Scale of Miles

The most famous explorers to reach the Northwest by land were Meriwether Lewis and William Clark. The United States had just bought a huge piece of land. It went from the Mississippi River to the Rocky Mountains. President Thomas Jefferson asked Lewis and Clark to explore the land, to see if there was a water route all the way across to the ocean, and to write about the natural resources they saw and the native people they met.

Lewis and Clark's long journey began near St. Louis, Missouri. From there, they took a group of men up the Missouri River in boats. They made other parts of their trip by foot, on horseback, and in canoes.

The men traded with many Native American tribes along the way. They made notes about the people they met and the plants and animals they saw.

The men spent their first winter in the land of the Mandan tribe. There they met a fur trader and his Native American wife, Sacagawea. The couple traveled with Lewis and Clark across the Rocky Mountains. They were guides and *interpreters*. Sacagawea carried her baby boy the whole way.

Sacagawea was a Shoshone who had been captured years earlier from her own tribe in Idaho. When the group reached Shoshone land, she helped the explorers get food and horses by trading with her own tribe.

The Northwest at Last

The last part of the journey, along the Columbia River, was especially hard. Just before the second winter came, the group reached the Pacific Ocean. They crossed the Columbia River and made their winter camp near where Astoria, Oregon, is today. They called it Fort Clatsop. In the spring, the explorers began the long trip home.

When they finally got home after two years, Lewis and Clark had learned much about the new lands and the Native Americans. They had collected plants, animal skins and bones, and Indian artifacts to take back to President Jefferson. They had even sent back a live prairie dog. They helped give the United States a stronger claim to the Northwest.

The Mandan people had never seen a dark-skinned person before. York was Clark's slave. He helped Lewis and Clark work with the Native Americans.

Journal Notes

Clark wrote these notes during the hard trip along the Columbia River:

November 5, Tuesday, 1805. *We met four canoes of Indians. . . . The day proved cloudy with rain. . . . We are all wet and cold.*

November 6, Wednesday, 1805. *The Indians of the two lodges we passed today came in their canoes. . . . I [got] two beaver skins for which I gave five small fish hooks. . . . Dried out our bedding and killed the fleas . . . in our blankets.*

November 7, Thursday, 1805. *A cloudy, foggy morning. Great joy in camp. We are in view of the ocean, this great Pacific Ocean that we have been [waiting] to see.*

Memory Master

Lesson
2

1. List three reasons Robert Gray's trip was important.

2. What body of water did George Vancouver explore?

3. Why did Lewis and Clark come to the Northwest?

4. What Indian woman went on the famous trip with Lewis and Clark?

5. List two things Lewis and Clark did that helped the United States.

*Beaver hair was soaked and pressed to make **felt.** This firm shiny felt was then shaped to make tall hats.*

FUR TRADING DAYS

Wild animals roamed the land and waters of the Northwest. One explorer saw "bears, wolves, foxes, deer, river otters, sea otters, raccoons, brown minks, beavers, wild cats, gray rabbits, squirrels, mice, and seals."

Many of the animals had thick furs. Fur trading became a big business in the region traders called "Oregon Country." Oregon Country was all the land that is now Oregon, Washington, Idaho, and part of British Columbia. It was a big place.

Beavers—Nature's Engineers

Sea otters were the first animals the explorers wanted. They were also the first that almost became extinct. The next important animals to be hunted for their furs were beavers.

Beavers are fascinating animals. They have long sharp teeth for cutting down trees. Tree bark is their favorite food. They have webbed feet for swimming. They use their flat tails as building tools.

What they build is amazing! They begin by cutting down small trees and dragging them to the center of a stream. They add more trees. Then they pile on dirt and stones to hold the sticks in place. This becomes a dam. It blocks the stream and forms a quiet pond.

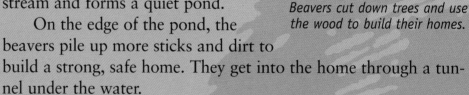

Beavers cut down trees and use the wood to build their homes.

On the edge of the pond, the beavers pile up more sticks and dirt to build a strong, safe home. They get into the home through a tunnel under the water.

Every summer, the beavers build and repair their homes and dams. They also cut down trees and drag pieces to the pond. These are stored under the water. In winter, the beaver family can drag in pieces of wood and eat the bark for food.

Thousands of beavers used to be found in forests all over Europe and North America. Then came the fur trade. In the 1800s, tall hats made of pressed beaver fur were very popular for men. Women wore fur collars on their clothes. Trappers killed so many beavers that the animals almost became extinct.

At Point Defiance Park in Tacoma, you can get an idea of what life was like at a fur trading fort.

LIFE AT A FUR TRADING FORT

Much of the work of trading for furs went on in forts. Forts were a group of buildings with a tall fence around them. The fence, or **stockade,** was made of strong logs—strong enough for **protection** in case of an Indian attack. There were many forts in the Northwest.

The leader of Fort Nisqually made these notes. They tell about the daily life at a fur trading fort.

December 23, 1833. Set all hands to work to collect fire-wood. A few Indians arrived but brought only two beaver to trade. Weather very cold.

December 25—Christmas day. I gave the men [food and drink] to make up in some measure for the bad living they have had all year. They enjoyed the feast.

This year's returns are:

1,038 large beaver
700 rats
190 raccoons
33 large black bear
13 small black bear
2 elk
1 sea otter
[and other animals]

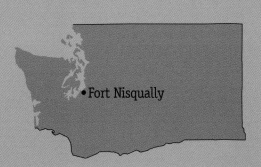

•Fort Nisqually

Explorers and Fur Traders

In this drawing of Fort Vancouver, can you find the stockade and the farms?

Fort Vancouver

Pieces of this vase were found at the site of Fort Vancouver. The vase is from China. How do you think it got to the fort?

THE HUDSON'S BAY COMPANY

There was a lot of money to be made by trapping and trading furs. The furs were sent to the big cities of America and across the ocean to Europe. American and English companies all wanted to control the fur trade. The biggest company was the Hudson's Bay Company. This English company played an important part in Washington's history.

The Hudson's Bay Company had forts in many places. Its *headquarters,* or main fort, was Fort Vancouver. It stood where Vancouver, Washington, stands today.

The officers of the company and their families lived inside the fort. Other workers lived outside. Many of the traders had Native American wives, but most of the people at the fort were men.

The fort was almost like a small city, with all kinds of business going on. Inside there were stores, workshops, and meeting rooms. Outside was a sawmill, a flour mill, and other buildings. There was a small school inside the fort.

There were also vast farmlands. There were fields of wheat, oats, and barley. There were fruit trees and vegetable gardens. There were hundreds of farm animals grazing nearby.

The Washington Adventure

The people who lived and worked for the Hudson's Bay Company came from many places. Most were English, Scottish, American, and French Canadian. Some were Native Americans.

Hawaiians also came. Some found work on fur trading ships that stopped in Hawaii. Others worked at forts in the Northwest. Several places were named for Hawaiians who lived here in fur trading times.

A Great Leader

The leader of the Hudson's Bay Company activities in Oregon Country was John McLoughlin. He ran the business of the company. He decided where the traders would go and how many goods to trade for furs. He made sure that Native Americans were treated fairly. He helped people in need. He was also a medical doctor. For many years, he was the most powerful person in the Pacific Northwest.

The Brigades

Each year, McLoughlin sent a large group of traders into the *wilderness* looking for furs. The group was known as a *brigade.* The men trapped and traded as they went.

They were a colorful group. There were traders from several countries and Native Americans of many tribes. Some men took their Native American wives along. The brigade leader wore a tall fur hat, a fancy shirt, and a long coat with gold buttons. The men often sang songs as they traveled.

John McLoughlin is sometimes called the Father of Oregon. Native Americans called him the White-Headed Eagle. Can you see why?

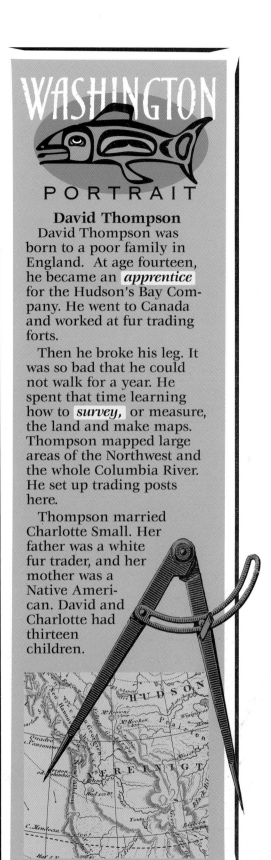

WASHINGTON
P O R T R A I T

David Thompson

David Thompson was born to a poor family in England. At age fourteen, he became an *apprentice* for the Hudson's Bay Company. He went to Canada and worked at fur trading forts.

Then he broke his leg. It was so bad that he could not walk for a year. He spent that time learning how to *survey,* or measure, the land and make maps. Thompson mapped large areas of the Northwest and the whole Columbia River. He set up trading posts here.

Thompson married Charlotte Small. Her father was a white fur trader, and her mother was a Native American. David and Charlotte had thirteen children.

This painting shows a mountain man and his Native American wife.

▲ Detail: *Setting Traps for Beaver.* Painting by Alfred Jacob Miller

MOUNTAIN MEN

The most famous fur traders in United States history were the mountain men. They worked and slept outside in all kinds of weather. Their food was simple. There were no stores to go to if they ran out of food, and no doctors to help them if they got sick. They walked and rode horses through the Rocky Mountains without roads or maps.

Work began in the fall. Every day, the mountain men set their traps. Sometimes they traveled many miles in one day to check them. They cleaned and dried the skins of the beavers they caught.

Some of the trappers worked alone. Others worked in groups. Some of the mountain men married Native American women, and the whole family worked together.

Mountain men worked until the heavy snows of winter. Some of them spent the winter with a Native American tribe.

The Washington Adventure

Some of the mountain men stayed in Oregon Country. But it was not easy for them to compete with the powerful Hudson's Bay Company. Many left to trap in other places.

Opening the Way for the Pioneers

The fur trade was important to Washington history for about sixty years. During that time, trappers and traders learned a lot about Oregon Country. They got to know the native people. They learned about the climate and natural resources. They explored the land and made some of the first maps of the Pacific Northwest. All these things would be important to the pioneers who would soon come to live here.

Linking the Past to the Present

Today, people protect animals in many ways. There are laws against killing animals that are in danger of becoming extinct. Hunters have to get permits to kill certain animals, and they can only hunt at certain times of the year. Special parks give animals a safe place to live.

Lesson
3

Memory Master

1. Which two animals were most important to the fur trade?

2. How did the people at the Hudson's Bay Company get food?

3. Who was John McLoughlin?

4. List three things that happened at a rendezvous.

5. What were some of the ways fur traders helped the pioneers who came later?

The Rendezvous

In spring, the trapping started again. In summer, when the animal fur was not as thick, trapping stopped. Then it was time for the *rendezvous.*

It was business and party, all in one. There was a lot of buying and selling. Trappers sold their furs to fur companies. They used the money to buy supplies. They might buy boots, blankets, tobacco, flour, coffee, gunpowder, and a knife or rifle. Native Americans also came to the event and traded furs, moccasins, clothing, and other things they had made.

Then came the fun. There were feasts, races, contests, storytelling, and gambling. By the end of the rendezvous, some trappers had spent all they earned.

The yearly events were held in the valleys of the Rocky Mountains. Painting by W. H. Jackson.

Chapter 3 Review

Activity

1. Trace Robert Gray's route on a globe. Remember, he had to sail south around South America in order to go from Massachusetts to the Pacific Northwest. On his way home to Boston, he sailed south of Asia and Africa and then crossed the Atlantic Ocean.

2. Do you think Vancouver was a good location for the Hudson's Bay Company to build its main fort? Write a few sentences about why the banks of the Columbia River might be a good place to build a fur trading fort.

Activity

Make a Timeline

What was going on in the rest of America while Europeans were exploring Oregon Country?

To find the answer, work with a group of classmates. You'll need an encyclopedia or U.S. history book, a long piece of paper, and two colors of markers.

1. First, find the dates of these important events in U.S. history:

   • Christopher Columbus arrives in North America.

   • Spain founds Santa Fe, New Mexico.

   • Pilgrims arrive in North America.

   • The War of Independence begins.

   • America fights England again in the War of 1812.

2. Next, make a timeline. Start with the year 1450 and end with the year 1850. Put a mark for every ten years in between.

3. Choose one color marker to write on the dates and the events above. Then use another color to write in some of the dates and events from the timeline at the front of this chapter on pages 60–61 What things happened at about the same time?

The Washington Adventure

What Happened First?

Write A, B, C down the side of a piece of paper, with three blank lines under each letter, just like you see below. Read the events, then number the events of each set 1, 2, or 3 for the order in which they happened.

A.

_____ American explorers came to the Northwest.
_____ Spanish explorers came to the Northwest.
_____ English explorers came to the Northwest.

B.

_____ Fur became the Northwest's most important natural resource.
_____ Robert Gray's men traded sea otter furs in China.
_____ Beavers and sea otters almost became extinct.

C.

_____ Fur traders built forts in the Northwest.
_____ Explorers came to the Northwest.
_____ Native Americans lived in the Northwest.

Fill in the Blanks

On a piece of paper, number from 1 to 4. Write the complete sentence, filling in the blanks.

1. _____ named the Columbia River and claimed the lands around it.
2. _____ explored and claimed Puget Sound.
3. _____ was the biggest fur trading company in the Northwest.
4. _____ explored the land from the Missouri River to the Pacific Ocean.

America or England?

Make two lists on a piece of paper. Label one list "America" and label the other list "England." On the first list, include all the people or facts that helped America claim parts of the Northwest. On the second list, write the things that helped England claim parts of the Northwest.

Write a sentence about the country you think had the strongest claim to the Northwest.

Be an Explorer

On a piece of paper, list all the reasons for exploring that you can find in this chapter. Now pretend that you are an explorer. Which reason would be the most important to you?

Write a few sentences telling why you would like to explore an unknown land.

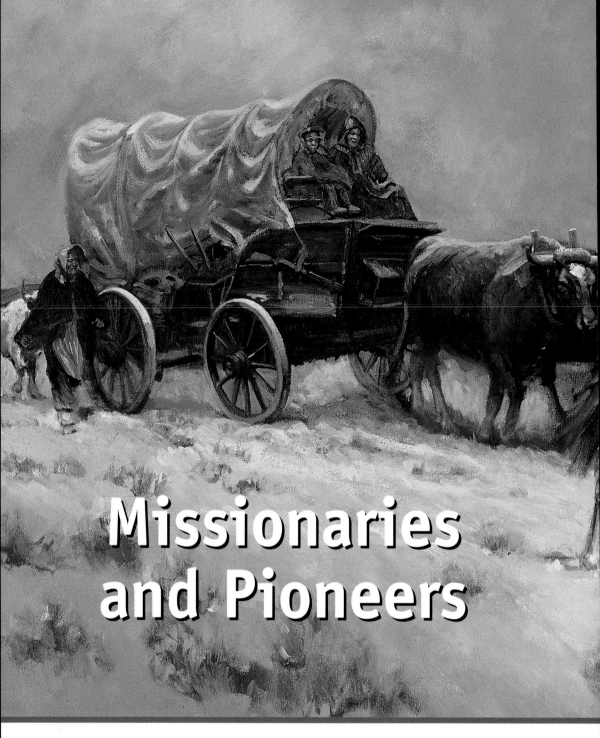

chapter 4

**THE TIME
1830-1880**

*Strong of heart and
brave of soul,
We marched and
marched to
reach the goal.*

From "Song of the Pioneers"

Missionaries and Pioneers

Timeline of Events

1831
Four Indian men go to St. Louis
to see William Clark.

1847
Marcus and Narcissa Whitman are murdered.

1845
First American settlers live in Washington.

1830   1840   185

1834
First missionaries arrive.

1844
George Washington Bush
family comes to
Oregon Country.

1846
Washington becomes part
of the United States.

Caught by Snow is a painting that shows a family on the Oregon Trail. Pioneers tried to leave early in the spring so they could get to Oregon before winter.

Painting by Glen Hopkinson

1856 Mother Joseph comes to the Northwest.

1877
Chief Joseph retreats.

1860

1870

1880

1854–1855
Washington
Indian treaties

1872
San Juan Islands become part of the United States.

81

Missionaries started schools, churches, and farms in many places.

The Missionaries

PEOPLE TO KNOW
Cayuse Indians
William Clark
Mother Joseph
Eliza Spalding
Henry Spalding
Marcus Whitman
Narcissa Whitman
Sager Children

PLACES TO LOCATE
St. Louis, Missouri
Lewiston, Idaho
Spokane
Vancouver
Walla Walla

WORDS TO UNDERSTAND
disease
orphanage
possession

MISSIONARIES COME TO THE INDIANS

During the fur trading years, a few visitors came to the Northwest. They saw the farms near the forts. They saw that Oregon Country was a good place to live. After they returned home, they wrote about what they had seen. They told their friends. Soon, many Americans were talking about moving to Oregon.

The first new settlers who came to stay were missionaries. They came here to teach their religion and way of life to the Native Americans.

Native Cultures Change

When fur traders came to the Northwest, the life of native people began to change. Hunting was no longer just a way of getting food. Indian hunters began killing animals to get their furs. They traded the furs for metal tools and other things they had never had.

These things brought more changes, and people could see that some of the changes were good. With metal knives and axes, Native Americans could carve wood more easily. Wool blankets were colorful and warm.

Native Americans believed that special *possessions* were often gifts from spirits. The fur traders had many wonderful things. This made native people wonder if the traders had powerful spirits. They began to wonder about the traders' religion.

Four Indian men went all the way to St. Louis to talk to Captain William Clark. They had heard about him when Lewis and Clark had visited the Northwest. They told Clark that they would like to learn about the white people's religion.

Churches heard about this request. Before long, missionaries headed to Oregon Country. The missionaries were the first Americans to build homes and stay in the Northwest.

Photo by Susan Myers

Visitors to the Whitman mission enjoyed the pond near the mission buildings.

THE WHITMANS

Among the early missionaries were a doctor named Marcus Whitman and his wife, Narcissa. They came west with another couple, Henry and Eliza Spalding. Narcissa and Eliza were the first white women to travel to the Northwest.

The Whitmans started a mission near today's city of Walla Walla. The Spaldings settled near the Nez Perce tribe near Lewiston, Idaho. These were two of the Protestant missions in the Northwest. Other missions were started, too. One was near Spokane. Each mission had homes, farms, a church, and a school.

Missionaries were either Protestants or Catholics. Catholics and Protestants had different ways of thinking about religion.

The Whitmans went to Fort Vancouver before starting their mission. Dr. McLoughlin was very kind to them. He gave them supplies. He also asked Narcissa to help teach music to his daughter and the other children.

"This morning I visited the school to hear the children sing. There were about fifty-one children, who have French fathers and Indian mothers. . . . English is spoken by only a few."

—*Narcissa Whitman, 1836*

This is part of a diary of Mary Richardson Walker, another missionary, in 1838:

Thursday, September 6.
Helped Mrs. Whitman a little in washing, sewed a little, put up seeds.

Sunday, September 9.
Prayer meeting in the morning. Then instruction to natives. Then sermon.

Monday, September 10.
Rose early. Worked hard as I could. . . . Oh dear, how I would like to be home about this time, and see brothers, hear from all the good folks! I wish I could have a letter from some of them!

Saturday, October 27.
For several days have been . . . fixing things. Today baked pies and hulled corn. Health good, weather fair.

Monday, October 30.
Washed, wrote a letter to Mother.

Sunday, November 4.
A long day for me. A day seems a week when my dear husband is [away].

The missionaries worked hard. Their days were filled with praying, teaching, farming, and doing many chores. Life was often lonely, far away from relatives and friends.

For the Whitmans, the saddest day was when their daughter drowned in the river near their home. She was only two years old.

Tragedy at the Whitman Mission

Dr. Whitman could see that the Northwest was a good place to live. He hoped many settlers would come, and he wanted to help them. The Whitmans proved that families could travel to Oregon Country and make a good life here. They gave food and medicine to settlers on their way west. They told them about the land and the people of the region. The mission became a welcome stop for travelers.

Marcus Whitman

Narcissa Whitman

The Cayuse Indians, however, were not happy to have so many settlers cross their land. Even worse, some fur traders and pioneers were sick with measles or smallpox. Many Indians died when they got the **diseases** from the white people.

Doctor Whitman worked hard, but he could not cure the people. Over half of the Cayuse tribe died. Some Cayuse men grew angry. They blamed Dr. Whitman for not making the people well. One day, a group of Cayuse attacked the mission. They killed the Whitmans and other people there.

Linking the Past to the Present

Measles and smallpox killed thousands of pioneers and Indians. Do people still get these diseases today?
What has been done to prevent them?

The Sager Children's Story

Catherine Sager was just nine years old when her family decided to go west. She had two older brothers and three younger sisters. Another baby sister was born on the trip.

Travel with a wagon train was pleasant for a while. The weather was fine. The Sagers shared happy times with other travelers in their group.

Then the troubles began. One day, Catherine got caught under their wagon and broke her leg. Then her parents got sick. First her father died, and later her mother died. The seven Sager children were alone.

Other adults took care of the children until they reached the Whitman mission. There, the children received a warm welcome and a happy surprise. Dr. and Mrs. Whitman adopted the whole family. The Whitmans' only child had died, and they were happy to have a family again.

The children studied at the mission school and helped with chores. They had three peaceful years.

Then trouble struck again. The Whitmans and some of the other people at the mission were killed. Only four sisters survived. When they grew up, they shared their memories in writing and speeches. Here is part of what Catherine wrote about mission life:

This drawing was made by a woman who stayed at the Whitman mission for a while.

Mrs. Whitman and the girls did the work in the summer. Each of us had her tasks. When the work was done, we all sat in a large room at our sewing, save one of us, who read aloud to the rest.

Supper was at 5 o'clock. In the spring, the evenings were spent in the garden putting in seeds; otherwise we did as we pleased. Sometimes the boys would bring horses for us to ride. At times we would go with the doctor to visit the lodges where the Indians were sick.

This doll once belonged to Catherine Sager. How is it different from dolls today?

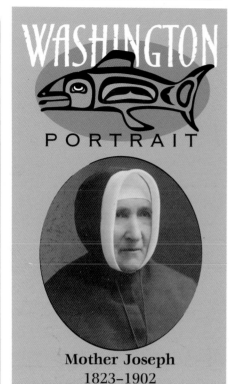

WASHINGTON
PORTRAIT

Mother Joseph
1823–1902

Esther Pariseau was a very talented young woman. At age twenty, she was already a skilled carpenter. But few jobs were open to women. In fact, the only place that she could work was in the Catholic Church. She became a nun.

For years, Esther worked with other nuns in Canada, near her family's home. She learned many skills, from nursing and gardening to running a business.

Later, Esther was sent to Vancouver, Washington. She received a new name—Mother Joseph. (The "mother" is in charge of the nuns.)

Mother Joseph started seven hospitals, twelve schools, and two *orphanages.* She helped build many of the buildings herself. She worked until she was almost eighty years old.

CATHOLIC MISSIONS

After the Whitmans were killed, many Protestant missions closed. Catholic missions stayed open, though. These missions were different. Catholic priests served the fur traders who were Catholic. They did not try to make big changes in the Indians' way of life. Instead, they taught Bible stories and prayers. As a result, Catholic missions were easier for the Indians to accept.

The best-known Catholic missionary in the Northwest came many years after the Whitmans. Her name was Mother Joseph.

Linking the Past to the Present

In our nation's capitol, each state has two statues of important people. Washington's statues are of Dr. Whitman and Mother Joseph.

What do you think

Missionaries tried to teach the Indians to live and think like the white settlers. They wanted them to read the Bible, plant crops, and speak English. They thought this would help the Indians. Missionaries often did not respect the Indian ways or spiritual beliefs.

Do you think people should try to teach their religion to other people if they think it would help them? Why or why not?

Lesson 1 — Memory Master

1. What changes to the Indians' way of life did the fur trade bring?

2. Why did some Native Americans want to learn about the explorers' religion?

3. What did missionaries hope to teach the Native Americans?

4. List two ways the Whitmans helped settlers.

5. List two things Mother Joseph did to help the people in the Pacific Northwest.

Parts of the Oregon Trail can still be seen today.

Photo by Susan Myers

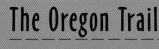

The Oregon Trail

PEOPLE TO KNOW
George Washington Bush
Isabelle Bush

PLACES TO LOCATE
Missouri
Willamette Valley
Bush Prairie
Rocky Mountains

WORDS TO UNDERSTAND
challenge
homestead
pioneer
slavery
wagon train

TRAVELING THE OREGON TRAIL

In those days, there were no roads or railroads leading to the Pacific Northwest. The first *pioneers* who wanted to move to Oregon Country had only one choice. They would have to make their own trail across America. The route became known as the Oregon Trail.

The Oregon Trail started in Missouri. The trail followed rivers most of the way. It went across the flat plains, then into the steep Rocky Mountains. The trail ended in the Willamette Valley. This valley is part of Oregon today.

Large groups of settlers traveled along the trail. They loaded their things into wooden wagons. One group followed another, making a long *wagon train.* The settlers' horses and cattle walked along behind. The whole group moved very slowly, often just twelve miles a day. (Today, you can travel twelve miles in twelve minutes by car.)

Missionaries and Pioneers

87

During the daytime, there was work to do. Children gathered firewood as the wagons moved slowly along. Some members of the wagon train rode off on horseback to hunt. If they were lucky, they might shoot a deer or a buffalo to eat. On other days, food, firewood, and water were hard to find.

At night, the wagons formed a large circle. In the center of the circle, each family built a fire and cooked a simple dinner. After eating, people often sang songs and shared stories. They slept in the wagons or on the ground. The next morning, after breakfast, they started walking again. This went on day after day, for as long as six months.

Follow the trail from Missouri to Oregon. What rivers did the trail follow? Find the Whitman mission where pioneers stopped to rest and get supplies. What fort was at the end of the trail?

The Oregon Trail

Columbia River

CANADA

Fort Vancouver
Columbia River
Whitman Mission
Walla Walla

Fort Boise

Snake River

Fort Hall

Independence Rock

Fort Bridger
South Pass

Fort Laramie

Platte River

Mississippi River

Missouri River

N
W   E
S

0   500 Miles

Scale of Miles

Missouri River

Teams of oxen, mules, or horses pulled the wagons west.

Danger on the Trail

The trip across the Oregon Trail was a brave adventure. But it was not easy! Every day, it seemed, there were problems and dangers to face.

There were hot and dusty weeks of walking under the burning sun. On other days it rained, and the wagons got stuck in the mud.

The land the pioneers crossed was home to different Indian tribes. Sometimes this was a problem, too. With so many travelers hunting wild animals for food, and so many cattle eating the wild grass, the native people worried that there would not be enough for everyone. Sometimes this led to fighting.

Crossing rivers was always a *challenge.* There were no bridges. Sometimes the travelers found a shallow place to walk across the river. Other times, they had to stop and build wooden rafts to carry the wagons. Many animals drowned in the swift water.

Crossing steep mountains was even harder. There were trees in the way that had to be chopped down. There were ditches that had to be filled. Sometimes there was no grass for the animals to eat. The travelers and their tired animals did the best they could. They tried to find low routes, called passes, through the mountain ranges. But with no roads, these crossings were always hard.

Why Did They Come?

Why did so many people make this long trip? The main reason was land. At the end of the Oregon Trail there was a great deal of good land. In Oregon Country, families could *homestead.* They could claim a piece of land, farm it, and own it for free. At first, every family that came to Oregon Country got a large piece of land for free. Later, when the best farmland was gone, new towns were good places to start a business.

Some people also came for the adventure. There was a chance to explore a beautiful new place.

Some wanted to get away from problems at home. One of those problems was *slavery.* At that time, half of the states still allowed slavery. Many pioneers, both black and white, dreamed of putting slavery far behind them.

Linking the Past to the Present

The time of the Oregon Trail was an important time in United States history. Today, the right to move to a new place to live and work is still an important American freedom. Has your family moved to Washington from another place?

A Woman's Point of View

Some women in the wagon trains kept diaries of their trips. Lydia Allen Rudd wrote these notes in 1852:

June 2. We have had a [hard] day. Our road has been sand hills. The sand six inches deep in places.

June 12. Passed five graves this morning and a camp where one of their men was dying.

August 14. Bought a salmon fish of an Indian today, weighing 7 or 8 pounds. Gave him an old shirt, some bread, and a sewing needle.

September 1. Traveled 14 miles today on the Blue Mountains. Climbed up and down the highest hills that I ever saw a person pass over. Very steep and rocky. No water for our [animals].

September 6. We have not been able to leave this miserable place today. I am not as well as yesterday, and no [doctor] to be had.

AN AFRICAN AMERICAN FAMILY

Bush Prairie

George Washington Bush had already lived a full life before he came to Oregon Country. He had been to school, fought in two wars, and was a rancher. His wife Isabelle, a white woman, had been a nurse.

Bush was a free African American in a slave state. It was not a safe and comfortable place to be. He hoped he could find a better life in the Pacific Northwest. With his wife and their sons, he decided to go west on the Oregon Trail.

George and Isabelle Bush and their children came to settle in the West.

When they arrived in Oregon Country, the Bush family got a sad surprise. Black settlers were not welcome in the Willamette Valley. The pioneers had just voted to keep them out.

The wagon train decided to head north and settle near Puget Sound. Bush and his family became the first African American pioneers to settle on land that later became part of Washington State.

Bush became known as a generous neighbor and a good farmer in Washington. When other settlers moved to the region, he gave them seeds and helped them start farms. He also got along well with the Native Americans who lived nearby. He helped give the United States a stronger claim to the land.

Bush's son was later elected to the first Washington State government. The place where the Bush family lived is now called Bush Prairie.

Packing Up

Imagine that you are leaving your home forever. You are moving to a place that has no stores and no hospitals. You must pack everything you will need into a wagon. Make a list of at least ten things you will take with you. Then compare your list to this list from the 1800s.

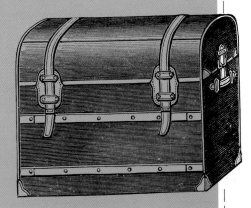

One pioneer said that travelers should bring these things:

flour	pots and kettles
cornmeal	rope
sugar	shovel
fruit	axe
butter	hammer
lard	water bucket
vegetables	soap
bacon	clothing
medicine	extra bedding
salt for animals	grease for wheels
rifle	

Can you think of other supplies you might need to take? Will you have room for them?

"We children, who had been in the wagon so many hours each day, waded the creek, made mud pies, and gathered posies."
—*Eliza Rogers*

"We sleep in our wagon on feather beds. We live on bacon, ham, rice, dried fruit, butter, bread, coffee, tea, and milk as we have our own cows. If some of the men kill an antelope we have a feast."
—*Sallie Hester, 1848*

Lesson 2

Memory Master

1. What famous trail did the pioneers use to get to Oregon Country?

2. How did children help their families on the long trip?

3. What were two problems the people had on the trail?

4. Why did people want to come to Oregon Country?

5. Why did the families of George Bush's wagon train go north and settle near Puget Sound?

A pioneer cabin was made of logs. The logs were stacked up like this. Mud between the logs kept out the cold winds.

Lesson 3

Pioneer Life

PLACES TO LOCATE
San Francisco, California
Seattle
Neah Bay

WORDS TO UNDERSTAND
difficult
provide
dense

THE HARD LIFE OF PIONEERS

The trip across the Oregon Trail was *difficult.* Yet it was only the beginning of hard work for the pioneers.

Once they got their land, pioneer families had to build their own homes and furniture. They cut down trees with simple tools. Then they split the logs into rough boards. The first houses they made were small wooden cabins. These often had no windows because there was no place to buy glass in Oregon Country.

In fact, there was no place to buy most of the things the pioneers needed. They could not buy stoves, so they built stone fireplaces for heating and cooking. They could not buy oil lamps, so they made candles. They made their own soap, too.

Pioneer families also *provided* all their own food. This meant clearing trees and rocks from the land so they could plant crops. This was very hard work. The families raised cows and made cheese and butter from the milk. They caught fish and killed other wild animals such as ducks, deer, and rabbits for meat.

Pioneer women made all the clothes for the family. They raised sheep, cut their wool, spun it into yarn, and wove it into cloth. They made shoes from animal skins.

Work and Play

All the work kept pioneer families very busy. Everyone had to help. Men cut wood, cleared land, and went hunting. Women cooked, cleaned, sewed, and cared for children. Even young children had chores.

For fun, the pioneers liked to tell stories. They also played guessing games and checkers. On special days, they had dances.

Memories of Childhood

Every pioneer family had a cow. People and animals drank the milk.

I was brought to Washington . . . by my parents in 1877. We came by train to San Francisco and by boat to Neah Bay. My father cooked in the Indian school. . . . He thought [this country] was the garden spot of the world.

He built a log house for the family, and I grew up there. I listend to wolves howling. They sometimes caught our sheep.

We rode horseback over trails, or walked, or rode in Indian canoes on the ocean. Once when I was sick, I was hauled out over the trail on a sled across the mountains.

—told by Jennie S. Tyler in *Told by the Pioneers*

This is one girl's memory of her first cabin:

It was a small log house . . . one room. My father had gotten some sacks of wheat. . . . My sister Annie and I slept on those sacks. They were cold. . . . [My father] got a load of lumber . . . and he made some chairs. He just took a piece of board and made them and then he cut down some birch trees and made the back and legs.

—told by Elsie Koehler Johnson in *Homestead Girlhoods*

Pioneer children played simple games outside:

Hide and seek in a dense jungle of young Douglas firs was most delightful; the great fir and cedar trees, logs and stumps, [gave] cover for any number of players.

This woman is using a spinning wheel to turn sheep's wool into yarn.

The teeter-board was available when the neighbor's children came. . . . The longest board that could be found was placed across a large log. A huge stone rested in the middle, and the children, boys and girls, little and big, crowded on the board, almost filling it. Then we carefully 'waggled' it up and down.

—told by Emily Inez Denny in *Blazing the Way*

The whole school sits on a huge tree stump. How many children are in the school? How old do you think the children are?

The Washington Adventure

After many years, the Baldridge School was left empty.

PIONEER SCHOOLS

One of the first things the settlers wanted was a school for their children. The schools were quite different, of course, from the ones most children attend today. The first schools were very small. Students of all ages shared a single room with one teacher. There were only a few books and a few homemade desks in the room.

Many students walked a long way to school. They carried their lunches in buckets or boxes.

Often the school year was only three to six months long. The rest of the time children were needed for work at home.

On weekends, the little schoolhouse became a meeting place. Church and Sunday schools were held there. Dances, plays, spelling bees, singing classes, and town meetings also took place at the school.

New Foods for Native Americans

Fur traders and pioneers brought new foods to the Northwest. Indian children tried them but did not always like them, as this boy said:

I first tasted potatoes, bread, vegetables, and other white men's food when I was ten years of age. Indian food is mostly fish, whale meat, sea lion, elk, deer, and bear. Cornflakes and fruit are the only food of the white man I like.

—told by William Mason in *Told by the Pioneers*

Lesson 3 — Memory Master

1. What did the pioneers use to build their homes?
2. How did the pioneers get food?
3. What did the children do for fun?
4. How were pioneer schools different from yours? How were they the same?
5. How was the food of Indian children different from the pioneers' food?

Changing Hands

PEOPLE TO KNOW
Chief Joseph
Chief Sealth

PLACES TO LOCATE
England
Germany
Canada
Willamette Valley
Puget Sound
Vancouver Island
San Juan Islands

WORDS TO UNDERSTAND
compromise
outnumber
reservation
surrender
treaty

San Juan Islands

WHO OWNED THE NORTHWEST?

Before the fur traders came, all the Northwest was Indian land. Later, the Hudson's Bay Company controlled the region's trade. This helped give England a strong claim to Oregon Country.

Then thousands of American pioneers settled on the rich farmland. Soon there were more American settlers than fur traders in this area. It was clear that this land would become part of the United States. However, England still had a strong claim to Puget Sound.

Washington Becomes Part of the United States

The United States wanted Puget Sound, and the president said he would go to war against England to get it. However, neither country really wanted to fight. Finally, they made an agreement. England would keep Vancouver Island and the land north of 49 degrees north latitude. This area later became part of Canada. The United States would keep the land to the south. This is the region we now call the Pacific Northwest.

Pigs, Potatoes, and Talk of War

The agreement left one thing unclear. Who owned the San Juan Islands? Both countries thought the islands should be theirs.

One day, an Englishman's pig walked onto a farm owned by an American. The pig ate some of the farmer's potatoes. The farmer complained, "Keep your pig on your own land!" The Englishman refused.

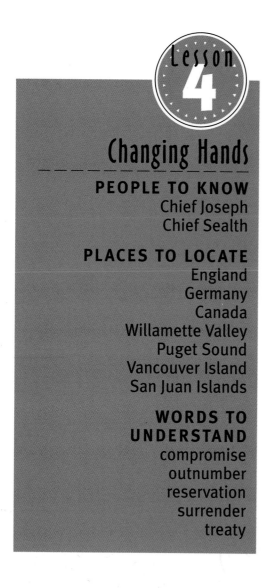

The American farmer shot the pig. Anger between the English and Americans grew stronger. Both nations sent soldiers to the islands. There was talk of war.

Instead of fighting, though, the countries asked the ruler of Germany to study the question and decide who should own the islands. The man listened to both sides. He decided that U.S. claims to the islands were stronger. Ever since then, the San Juan Islands have been part of Washington.

What do you think?

There are many ways to solve a problem between two countries or two people:

- One way is to fight. It causes more anger. Both sides usually get hurt.
- Another way is for both sides to talk together. People decide what to do without fighting. They each have to give up part of what they want. This is called **compromise.**

Which way of solving a problem do you think is best? Can you think of other ways to solve problems?

> **"You talk of offering goods for land. . . Goods and the earth are not equal."**
>
> —*Peo-Peo-Mox-Mox,*
> *Chief of the Walla Walla tribe*

NATIVE AMERICANS RESPOND

Most Native Americans had been friendly to the fur traders and early pioneers. But the pioneers brought problems. They took fish and hunted animals that Indian people depended on for food. The pioneers claimed land, put fences around it, and kept other people away. This included land where Indian families had lived and hunted each year. The pioneers also brought new diseases, and many Indians died.

Some Native Americans decided to fight. They attacked settlers who crossed their land. Some went to war to protect their way of life.

Other tribes made a different decision. They saw that more and more settlers were coming each year. "We will soon be *outnumbered,*" they said. "It is better to make peace."

Most Washington tribes signed *treaties* with the U.S. government. In the treaties, the government promised the Indians blankets, clothes, flour, tools, and money. The tribes promised to sell some of their land and move to places set aside for them. The places were called *reservations.* In return, the government promised that the tribes could still hunt and fish for food and live in peace. The government wanted the Indians to farm, and to send their children to school.

During Indian wars, the pioneers built strong log blockhouses. They were safe places to be during an attack.

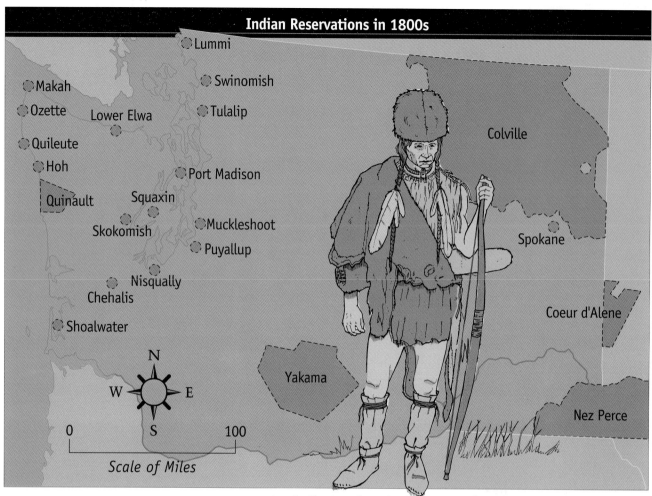

Indian Reservations in 1800s

Lummi
Makah
Swinomish
Ozette
Lower Elwa
Tulalip
Quileute
Hoh
Port Madison
Colville
Quinault
Squaxin
Skokomish
Muckleshoot
Puyallup
Spokane
Nisqually
Chehalis
Shoalwater
Coeur d'Alene
Yakama
Nez Perce

N W E S

0   100

Scale of Miles

In the treaties, the tribes agreed to give up some of their land.
They promised to move to places that were reserved for them.

Chief Sealth was a friend of the settlers.
Seattle was named after him.

CHIEF SEALTH

Two great Native American leaders were among those who made different decisions. Chief Sealth was one of them. He was a leader of the Suquamish and Duwamish tribes. He was known as a friend of the settlers.

Like most of the Coastal leaders, Chief Sealth decided to sign a treaty. He gave a speech at the treaty ceremony that later became famous.

The settlers are many. They are like the grass that covers vast prairies. My people are few. You say you will buy our lands and give us enough to live on. . . . We will accept your offer. But to us, the land of our ancestors will always be special. Every hillside, every plain and forest is filled with their spirits. The white man will never be alone. Our spirits will always be here.

The Washington Adventure

CHIEF JOSEPH

Giving up land was not as easy for Plateau people as it was for the Coastal tribes. Coastal people were used to living in small villages. The treaties allowed them to leave the reservations and go fishing each year as they always had. For them, it seemed that old ways of life could still go on. This was not true on the plateau. There, food was harder to find. Without their hunting lands, the people might not survive.

Chief Joseph was a leader of the Nez Perce, a Plateau tribe. The Nez Perce were peaceful people. They had been friendly with Lewis and Clark and with missionaries. The Spaldings' mission was on their land.

Then gold was found on Nez Perce land. More miners and more settlers were coming every day, and they wanted the Nez Perce to leave. The army told Chief Joseph's people they had to go.

Chief Joseph still wanted peace, but some of the young men did not. They did not want to move to a reservation far from where they lived. They wanted to fight or escape.

Chief Joseph made his decision. He wanted only peace, but he would help his people escape to Canada. The Nez Perce headed north. Women, children, and old people walked with the young men. The U.S. Army followed. There were many battles. The Nez Perce won many of them. But winter was coming. The people were cold and there was little food. Just before the Nez Perce reached the border, the army attacked. Many members of the tribe were killed.

Chief Joseph had no choice but to **surrender.** He said:

> My *heart is sick and sad. From where the sun now stands, I will fight no more forever.*

Chief Joseph tried to lead his people to Canada, but they were stopped by the U.S. Army. He died on the Colville Indian reservation.

A man, a boy, and a dog walk on the wooden sidewalk in Seattle about 150 years ago.

The Washington Adventure

The End of Pioneer Times

There had been other Indian wars in Washington, but Chief Joseph's was the last. When that war ended, pioneer times were ending. Seattle and Walla Walla were beginning to look like young cities, and other towns were growing, too. Still, there was plenty of wilderness between them. In some parts of Washington, a trip into town was still a rare adventure.

Compare this photo of early Seattle with pictures of Seattle in Chapter 1. How have things changed?

Memory Master

Lesson 4

1. Who lived in the Pacific Northwest before the fur traders came?

2. Which two countries claimed Puget Sound and the San Juan islands?

3. What did the tribes promise in the treaties? What did the government promise?

4. Who were Chief Sealth and Chief Joseph? Tell two things you learned about each one.

5. Why didn't the Nez Perce want to move onto a reservation?

Chapter 4 Review

Activity

Write a Speech

Pretend you are a Native American leader.
Pioneers are settling on the land where your family lives, hunts, and gathers food. You try to be friendly at first. You are interested in trading furs and fish for metal tools and glass beads. Then you see pioneers moving on more and more of your hunting lands. Your people get diseases they have never had before.

Write a speech you would give to the settlers. Explain how you feel.

Activity

What's For Dinner?

Imagine that you were a pioneer, living in the same area where you live today. What foods might you eat?

First, copy the foods that pioneers brought from the list on page 91. Then think about the wild plants and animals in your area that you might eat. What foods could you grow? Add these to your list. Then add all the foods you could get from the family's cow.

Now make a menu. Using only foods from your list, write or draw what you might eat for breakfast, lunch, and dinner.

Geography Tie-In

Read this description of a pioneer family's journey from their home in Seattle to visit their grandparents in Oregon. Trace their route on a map of Washington and Oregon in an atlas. Then find the route you could take to make this same trip today.

When the day came, in the long dark canoe, manned by a crew of Indians, we [started for] Olympia. . . . It was March of 1858, and it was chilly traveling on the big salt water. . . .

At the break of day, we paddled away until Stetchas was reached. Stetchas is the Indian name for Olympia. It means "bear's place."

From there, the mail stage awaited us. . . . The wagon sank up to its hub in black mud. . . . The long rough ride ended on the Cowlitz River. . . . Another canoe trip, this time on a swift stream, was safely made to Monticello.

A tiny steamboat carried us across the great Columbia, with its sparkling waves, and up the winding Willamette River to Portland, Oregon. The journey went to Oregon City [by boat] and then in a wagon [to the farm nearby].

The Washington Adventure

Pioneer Songs

Songs can be read like poems. Read this song, then write a verse about what you think pioneer children your age might have felt as they walked across the trails to Washington. Or, write a poem or a song about what adventures you might have had on the long trip!

Whenever I Think About Pioneers
Della Provost, A. Laurence Lyon

1. (Boys)

Whenever I think about pioneers,
I think of brave women and men.
I like to remember that children came, too,
I would like to have been a child then.

2. (Girls)

Yes, I'd like to have played all the games that they played,
And joined in their fun,
And I'd like to have slept under bright starry skies
When each day's measured journey was done.

3. (Boys)

I would like to have hunted for rabbits and deer,
Herded cattle and known all the joys
Of riding along in the wind and the sun,
As did most of the pioneer boys.

4. (Girls)

It would seem like a picnic to join with the girls
In each family chore.
And I think that I'd like a ceiling of sky,
And the green prairie grass for a floor.

THE TIME
1848-1900

In the 1800s, the fastest way to travel was by horseback or boat. As time went on, inventors worked on making a way to travel without animals that pulled a cart or wagon. They made steam engines that ran boats and trains. No longer did horses have to do all the work!

Washington Becomes a State

Timeline of Events

1853 Washington Territory is created.

1848
Oregon Territory is created.

1859 Oregon becomes a s

1861-65
United States
Civil War

1840

1850

1860

1848
Gold is found in California.

1855 Gold is found in eastern Washington.

1860 Mullan Road is completed.

*Trains carried
the heavy logs
to the sawmills and
the shipping ports.*

1883 First railroad comes to Washington.

1896 Gold is found in Alaska and Canada.

1870   **1880**   **1890**   **1900**

1869 First cross-country railroad is finished in Utah.

1885-86
Riots against Chinese
in Tacoma and Seattle

1889
Washington becomes a state.

This early mining town is in the foothills of the Rocky Mountains.

Lesson 1

Washington Territory

PEOPLE TO KNOW
May Arkwright Hutton
Isaac Stevens

PLACES TO LOCATE
Idaho
Montana
California
San Francisco, California
Walla Walla
Olympia
Port Townsend
Cascade Mountains
Puget Sound

WORDS TO UNDERSTAND
civil war
gold rush
millionaire
population
restaurant
territory

GOLD AND GROWTH

The year was 1849. Gold had been found in California the year before. Thousands of people called "forty-niners" were heading there, hoping to become rich. The *gold rush* had begun. California was booming. Its *population* was growing fast.

Washington's towns were still very small. But more people in California helped the Northwest grow, too.

The city of San Francisco, California, was a shipping port. The people there needed lumber to make shipping docks and buildings. Washington had plenty of forests with big, tall trees. Soon, ships loaded with logs were making trips between San Francisco and Puget Sound. Logging was big business.

Little by little, lumber and shipping towns sprang up around the Sound. Olympia, Port Townsend, Seattle, and Tacoma began to grow.

Then exciting news arrived from east of the Cascades. Gold and silver had been found there, too! Hopeful miners hurried east to places that are now in eastern Washington, Idaho, and Montana. Many miners stopped in the little town of Walla Walla to buy supplies. It became the largest town in the region.

Logging

Early loggers had no machines to help them. All the power came from people and animals. Two men worked on a tree. They started the cut with axes. One man stood on each side of a tree. Then each man pulled his end of a giant saw. Back and forth they sawed until the tree was ready to fall. After the tree crashed to the ground, ox teams hauled the logs out of the forest.

This is how we worked, Rud and Me. I chopped from the left, Rud from the right. Then each swung from the hips with the axe. Shunk-shink! Shunk-shink! Then we began to saw timber.

The huge old trees in Northwest forests were thick near the ground. The loggers made platforms to stand on. Then they could cut through a higher part of the tree that was more narrow.

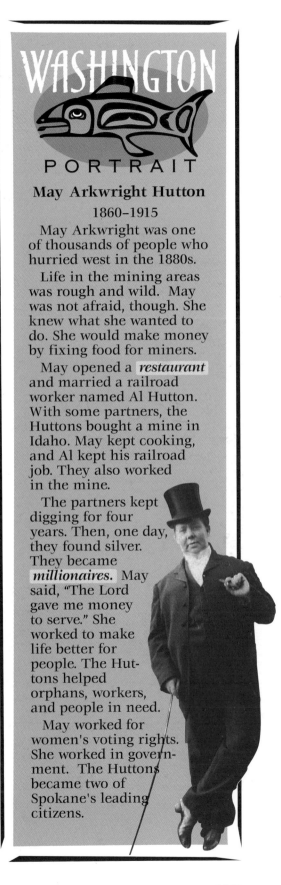

WASHINGTON
PORTRAIT

May Arkwright Hutton
1860–1915

May Arkwright was one of thousands of people who hurried west in the 1880s.

Life in the mining areas was rough and wild. May was not afraid, though. She knew what she wanted to do. She would make money by fixing food for miners.

May opened a **restaurant** and married a railroad worker named Al Hutton. With some partners, the Huttons bought a mine in Idaho. May kept cooking, and Al kept his railroad job. They also worked in the mine.

The partners kept digging for four years. Then, one day, they found silver. They became **millionaires.** May said, "The Lord gave me money to serve." She worked to make life better for people. The Huttons helped orphans, workers, and people in need.

May worked for women's voting rights. She worked in government. The Huttons became two of Spokane's leading citizens.

Coal Mining

Gold and silver were not the only minerals. Many people also worked in coal mines. The miners came from many countries. Even children found work sorting pieces of coal.

Coal became even more important after steam engines were invented. As coal burned, it heated up water in a tank. When the water boiled, steam shot up and made the engines turn. This kind of engine turned the wheels on steamships and trains.

People burned coal from this mine to warm their homes and cook their food.

A New Road

Getting in and out of Walla Walla was still hard. There was still no road across the Rocky Mountains. The army needed a road so soldiers and supplies could move faster between forts. The government built a road from Walla Walla into Montana. It was called the Mullan Road after the man in charge of building it.

The tracks of the old Mullan Road can still be seen.

Men chopped down huge trees and cleared away bushes. Mules dragged heavy logs over the ground to smooth out the road. It was not very wide, and it was closed by snow in the winter. But it was the only road across the mountains, and soldiers, settlers, and gold seekers were grateful for it. It made their trip much easier.

The Washington Adventure

TWO TERRITORIES

The little pioneer towns had logging and mining jobs. They were slowly starting to grow. Now families wanted things like roads and schools. They wanted an army to help keep them safe.

The settlers sent letters to United States' leaders, asking for help. The leaders listened. They created Oregon Territory. This was the first United States government in the Northwest.

At first, Oregon Territory was huge! All of Oregon Country was part of it. After a few years, it was divided. Washington Territory was made. The settlers here were happy. Now they had a government closer to home.

A *territory* is ruled by leaders who are chosen by the government in the nation's capital.

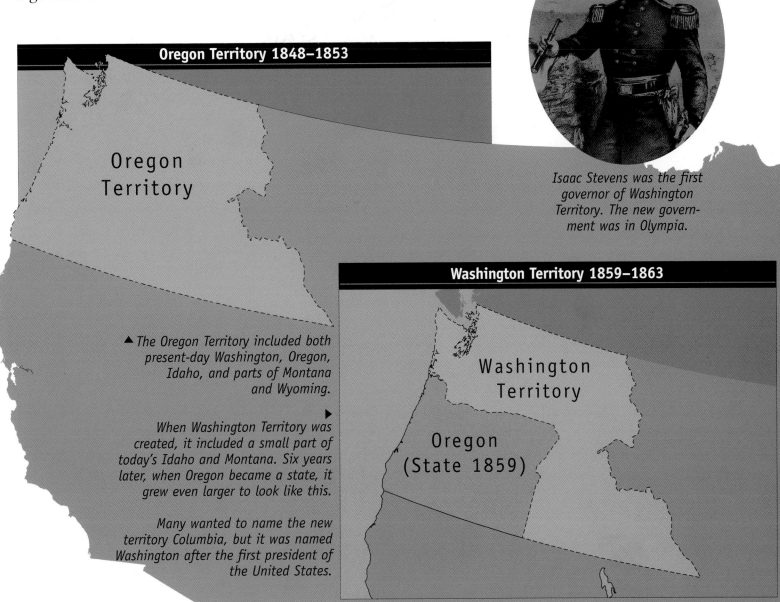

Isaac Stevens was the first governor of Washington Territory. The new government was in Olympia.

Oregon Territory 1848–1853

Oregon Territory

Washington Territory 1859–1863

Washington Territory

Oregon (State 1859)

▲ *The Oregon Territory included both present-day Washington, Oregon, Idaho, and parts of Montana and Wyoming.*

When Washington Territory was created, it included a small part of today's Idaho and Montana. Six years later, when Oregon became a state, it grew even larger to look like this. ▶

Many wanted to name the new territory Columbia, but it was named Washington after the first president of the United States.

Washington Becomes a State

A CIVIL WAR

While the Northwest was growing, the United States was going through one of the most terrible times in its history. The Civil War was going on. A *civil war* is when people from the same country fight against each other. States that allowed slavery were fighting against states that did not. The slave states of the South wanted to start their own country. President Abraham Lincoln led the struggle to keep the United States from breaking apart.

Washington was far from the war, but the war was important here. Some people came here to escape the problems of slavery. Others left to fight in the war. Isaac Stevens, the first governor of the territory, was one of the people who left. He was killed in a Civil War battle.

While the government was busy with war, there was little time to think about the territories. The people out west had to wait until the war was over.

Lesson 1

Memory Master

1. Why did many people rush to California in 1849?

2. What Washington resource was needed in San Francisco?

3. What was coal used for?

4. Who was the first governor of Washington Territory?

5. Why were settlers happy when Washington Territory was made?

RAILROADS ACROSS THE NATION

There were already many railroads in the East, but the people wanted to travel by train all the way across the country. After many years of hard work, the first cross-country railroad was built from Nebraska all the way to San Francisco. Settlers could take a train to San Francisco and then take a ship to Puget Sound. This was much easier and faster than the trip by wagon across the Oregon Trail.

Still, Northwest settlers wanted their own railroad. Trains would bring new settlers to the region. The railroads would also bring things the settlers needed, such as cooking stoves, window glass, and cloth.

Finally, a railroad was built to the Northwest. It was called the Northern Pacific. The tracks ran from Minnesota to Portland and then north to Tacoma.

The other towns on Puget Sound all wanted a railroad, too. The people of Seattle were angry that the tracks ended at Tacoma. They decided to build their own tracks. However, they soon found that this was hard work. They gave up after building just a small part. Ten years later, the people in Seattle got their wish. A new railroad, the Great Northern, came to Seattle.

Railroads Bring Growth

PEOPLE TO KNOW
James J. Hill

PLACES TO LOCATE
Europe
Asia
China
Japan
Canada
Minnesota
Nebraska
Oregon
Olympia
Seattle
Tacoma
Ellensburg
Spokane

WORDS TO UNDERSTAND
cannery
dynamite
prejudice
riot
spike

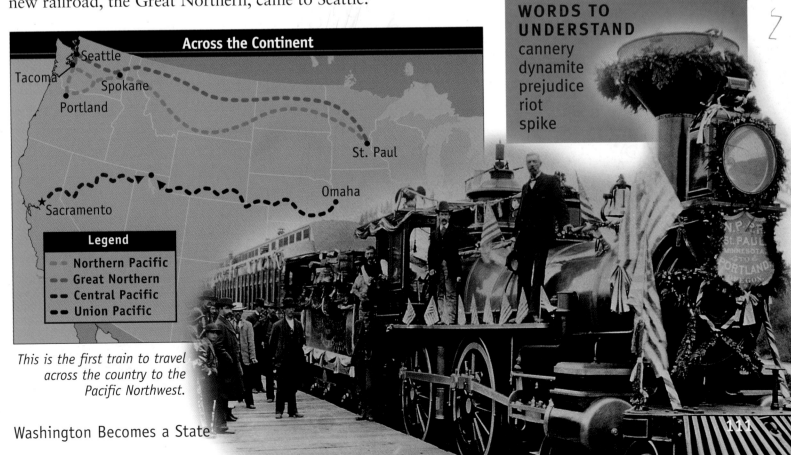

Across the Continent

Seattle
Tacoma
Spokane
Portland
St. Paul
Sacramento
Omaha

Legend
- - - Northern Pacific
- - Great Northern
- - Central Pacific
- - Union Pacific

This is the first train to travel across the country to the Pacific Northwest.

Washington Becomes a State

111

James J. Hill
1838–1916

As a boy in Canada, James Hill wanted to be a doctor. An accident left him blind in one eye, so he gave up that dream. He went to work in a store. Later, he moved to Minnesota and went to work on a steamboat. Soon, he owned his own shipping business.

Hill began buying and building railroads. He went on to run the Great Northern Railway Company. The railroad helped bring new settlers to the Northwest. It helped industry grow. James Hill became an important person in our state's history.

Horses hauled the heavy rails and ties to the work site.

Working on the Railroad

Thousands of workers helped build the great railroads of the West. They came from Europe, Asia, and many parts of the United States. They worked ten hours a day in the burning heat of summer and the freezing cold of winter.

Building a railroad was hard work. Everything had to be done by hand. Railroad workers used picks, shovels, and plows to make a flat path. They built bridges over rivers and blasted tunnels through the mountains with *dynamite.* The work was dangerous. Many men got hurt.

Next, workers laid the ties. Ties were heavy bars of wood, eight feet long. Across these, the men placed heavy iron rails. Finally, they pounded long thick nails called *spikes* into the rails to keep them on the ties. Think of pounding spikes with heavy hammers for ten hours!

CHINESE WORKERS FIND PREJUDICE

One of the largest groups of railroad workers came from China. Many people in China were very poor. News of the California gold had caused great excitement. "There's a mountain of gold in America!" people said.

Thousands of Chinese men came to America. They hoped to earn money to take home to their families in China.

The first men to arrive from China went to look for gold. However, Chinese workers met with *prejudice* in America. The good gold mining areas were closed to them. So were good jobs. Chinese men had to find other ways to earn a living. Some of them started a small business. Some cooked or washed and ironed clothes for other people. Many more went to work for the railroads.

After laying the tracks to California, many Chinese workers helped build the railroads of the Northwest. Others worked in mines. Some worked in fish *canneries.* They cleaned the fish and put them into cans. It was cold, smelly work.

Each year, new workers came, and others returned to China. While they were here, most lived in places that came to be called "Chinatowns."

Men work on the railroad in the Cascade Mountains during winter. The men in wide hats are Chinese.

The Chinese opened stores like this one in Seattle's Chinatown.

Chinese workers were paid less than other workers were, even if they did the same job.

Riots and Laws

The Chinese worked long hours for low pay. Other workers saw this. They feared the bosses would want more Chinese workers and that white workers would lose their jobs.

When times were bad and there were few jobs, many white people grew angry. There were *riots* against the Chinese in Tacoma and Seattle. A law was passed. It said that no more Chinese workers could come to the United States.

Washington Becomes a State

The First Japanese Immigrants

After the laws stopped the Chinese from coming to the United States, bosses looked for workers in Japan. Japanese men filled many of the jobs that Chinese workers had done for the mines, railroads, and fish canneries.

Like the Chinese, Japanese workers got low pay for hard work. One young man wrote:

> My work was to cut down trees or to build the railroads, digging and filling land in the mountains. It was hard work. I was only a boy of a little more than fifteen.
>
> Since I had never done hard labor, when I worked ten or twelve hours a day, the next morning, I couldn't open my hands. For two or three months, I dipped them in hot water to stretch the fingers back to normal, and sometimes I secretly cried.
>
> I had good reason to work my hardest . . . for when I left Japan, I had promised my mother, I'll surely come back to Japan in a year.

A Japanese family poses for a picture in their new country.

Picture Brides

After they had saved a little money, many Japanese men began to think about getting married. At that time, it was common for families in Japan to choose husbands or wives for their older children. The single men in America wrote home and asked their families to arrange a marriage. The women came to America on ships.

A man got a photo of the woman his family had chosen. When the ship came from Japan, the man picked out his new wife from the photo.

These "picture brides" worked as hard in America as their husbands did. Many Japanese families started farms. They worked planting and picking vegetables to sell in the cities. Strawberries were one of their most important crops. Japanese Americans were also the first to grow oysters in Washington's bays.

STATEHOOD AT LAST, 1889

Washington finally had enough people to become a state! It was something the settlers had wanted for a long time. People celebrated with parades and dances. They gave speeches. They hung banners and flags on buildings.

In a territory, the president of the United States chooses the top leaders. In a state, the people who live there vote for government leaders. Washington's people wanted to vote for their own leaders. The first task of these new leaders was to write rules for the new state. You can learn more about our state government in Chapter 9.

Washington was the 42nd state. How many states do we have today?

Washington
(State 1889)

Oregon
(State 1859)

Idaho
Territory

Fire!

The year Washington became a state was also a year of fires. Huge fires burned down the wooden buildings in Seattle, Spokane, and Ellensburg. On a hot, dry day in Seattle, a painter was heating glue in his shop. The pot boiled over and some of the glue caught fire. Fire spread through the shop. Winds carried it from one wooden building to the next. The fire jumped across the street. Soon entire blocks were on fire.

It was a sad time for the people who lost so many homes and work places. Some worked in tents until new brick buildings were made.

• Seattle   Spokane •

• Ellensburg

Lesson
2

Memory Master

1. Why did settlers want a railroad? Give at least three reasons.

2. Why did Chinese men come to America?

3. Give two examples of the prejudice that Chinese workers faced.

4. What was a picture bride?

5. Why did the settlers want Washington to become a state?

The trip to America was long and hard. The people went up to the top deck to get fresh air.

Lesson 3

A New Life in the Cities

PEOPLE TO KNOW
Edward Saloman

PLACES TO LOCATE
Scandinavia—Norway, Sweden, Denmark
Great Britain—England, Scotland, Wales, northern Ireland
Germany
Russia
Italy
France
Greece
Croatia
Canada
Alaska
Poulsbo
Aberdeen
Conway
Yakima

WORDS TO UNDERSTAND
automobile
elevator
immigrant
invention
outhouse
streetcars

A LAND OF OPPORTUNITIES

There were many reasons to move to Washington. There were plenty of jobs. A family could start a new business. They could get good farmland for a low price. The climate was mild and it was a pleasant place to live.

Most of the new settlers came from the United States and Canada. Many also came from Europe. If you had lived in Europe in the late 1880s, you probably would have heard many stories about America. You might have friends or family members who had moved here.

Many people in Europe were poor. They couldn't find jobs or good land for farming. They often faced prejudice because of their religion or their ideas about government. America was a place of land and jobs and freedom. Millions of *immigrants* came to the United States.

What do you think?

- Are you an immigrant? Did you move to America from another place?
- If you had to leave home and move to another country, how would you feel? What things about your homeland would you miss?

More People Come

The largest group of early European immigrants to Washington came from Scandinavia. This region includes Norway, Sweden, and Denmark. The land around Puget Sound reminded the people of home. Many settled in the fishing town of Ballard, which later became part of Seattle. Poulsbo is one of the Puget Sound places with a Norwegian name. One settler said, "Of all the states, Washington is the one best suited for Scandinavians."

The next largest group of immigrants were people from Ireland and Great Britain. This region included England, Scotland, and Wales. The people found jobs in cities and mines. They named some of the cities. For example, Aberdeen is named for a city in Scotland. Conway is a name from Wales.

Germans were the third largest group to arrive. Some became bankers and business leaders in cities. Some farmed in eastern Washington.

Other families came from Russia, Italy, France, Greece, and Croatia.

John Delco left Italy for America. He and his wife, Mary, lived near Renton with their six children.

Edward Saloman was an early governor of Washington Territory. He was from a Jewish immigrant family.

An Italian Boy's Story

The trip to America was not easy, as this boy wrote:

We had no idea what was in store for us. We were loaded onto a mule and taken to the train. We went aboard an [old ship]. We had left the Old Country. We were moving slowly toward a New World. We were packed in filthy bunks like herring [fish] in a barrel. All our things were crowded in there with us—even the tin dishes in which we ate the awful food we were served.

China
Japan
Canada
United States
Norway
Sweden Finland
Denmark
Russia
England Poland
Ireland Germany
Italy
Greece

John Nordstrom

John Nordstrom came to America from Sweden at the age of sixteen. He traveled through many states, working in mines, forests, and farms. Then he spent two hard years in Alaska, looking for gold. He didn't find any.

Nordstrom was tired of hard work for low pay. He decided to go to business college. After that, he and a friend opened a shoe store in Seattle. The little store grew slowly, but finally made money. Nordstrom and his partner opened more stores. Today, Nordstrom department stores can be found in cities around the United States.

Making a New Home

Making a new home in America was not easy. Most of the immigrants did not speak English. They had little money and knew little about American life.

Immigrants who spoke the same language and had the same culture helped each other. Many groups built churches, temples, or other gathering places. Some of these centers can be found today. They help keep cultures alive.

After a time, most of the people learned English. They became Americans. But they did not want to forget the good things about their homelands. They kept their foods, religion, songs, and art. They shared them with family and friends.

Jewish families came from Germany and other countries.

Let's Play!

Immigrant children learned English much faster than their parents did. They also learned American games. When they were not working or going to school, boys played baseball. If they didn't have a ball and bat, they played stickball. The bat was a stick or a broom handle. Knowledge of baseball heroes and rules was the badge of a true American.

One woman later wrote:

Sometimes we girls watched the boys play their games. We girls played only girls' games. We played hopscotch, only it was called "potsy." Mama didn't like me to play potsy. Hopping on one foot and pushing the thick piece of tin, I wore out a pair of shoes in a few weeks!

Neither my friends nor I played much with dolls. We all had plenty of little brothers and sisters to play with, and dolls were expensive.

African Americans Find Work

The first large group of African Americans came by train. They came to work in the mines in the Cascade Mountains. Some helped build railroads. Others worked on the ships that sailed up and down the Columbia River and along the coast. Later, many lived in cities. Some started small businesses.

Here, as in the rest of the United States, African Americans found prejudice. They were not allowed to live in many neighborhoods. They were kept out of most jobs. They had to sit in the back or in the balcony in theaters. They could not eat in restaurants or stay in hotels.

Still, some African Americans lived better here than in many other states. Some had nice homes in the cities. Some owned farms. Like other groups, they helped each other.

▼ Photo by Asahel Curtis

African Americans and other men walked to work and then rode a train to the mines.

Activity

Immigrants in Your Family

1. Learn as much as you can about where your family's ancestors lived. Locate the places on a world map.

2. Make two lists: "Washington People in the 1890s" and "Our Class." Under each list, write the countries people have come from.

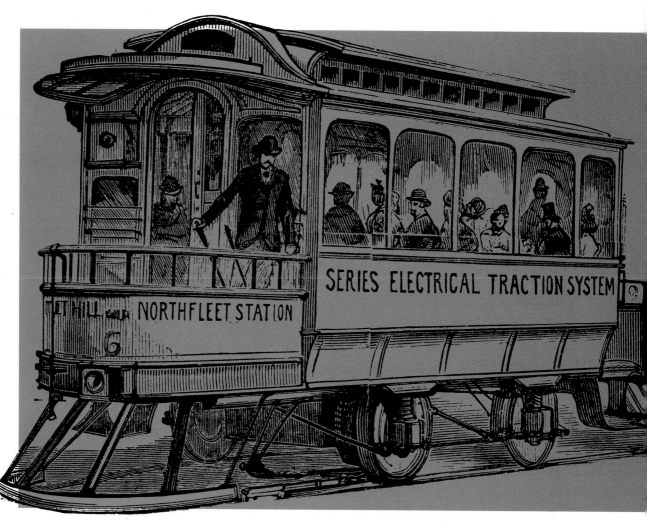

SERIES ELECTRICAL TRACTION SYSTEM

NORTHFLEET STATION

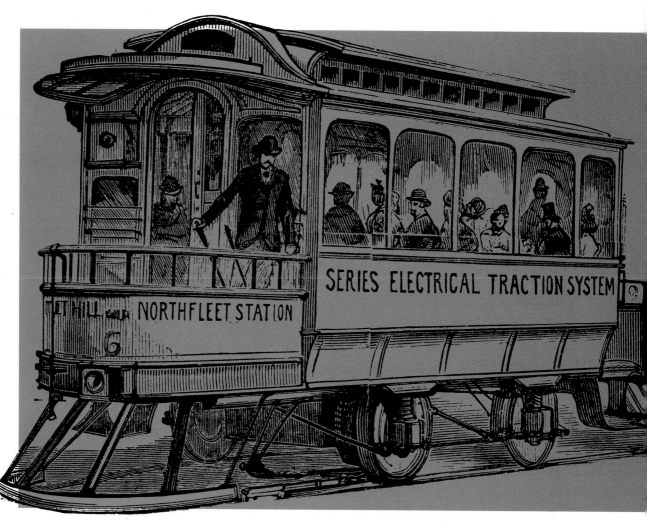

The first washing machines were hand-powered.

INVENTIONS MAKE LIFE EASIER

At the end of the 1800s, people were proud of their new state. They were also proud of the new *inventions* that were changing the way people lived. Electric lights were new. Indoor bathrooms replaced *outhouses* in more and more places. On the farms, though, most people still had oil lamps for light and used the wooden outhouses.

Inventions in the Cities

Inventions changed the look of cities. With new electric *elevators,* buildings could be taller. Electric streetlights made city streets bright. Spokane was one of the first western cities to have them.

In the East, people were starting to use a new invention—the telephone. It took a while longer for people in Washington to get telephones.

Transportation was changing, too. Horses pulled the first *streetcars.* Once in a while, the horses got scared and ran away with the car! Electric streetcars soon followed. They ran on tracks and got power from electric lines that were strung above the trains. People rode the streetcars in Seattle, Tacoma, Yakima, and other growing cities.

Then came the *automobile.* The first cars did not always run very well. There were no traffic lights and no stop signs. When it rained, the dirt roads got muddy. It was hard to drive in the mud.

Some people loved the new cars. Other people did not. They thought that twenty miles an hour was just too fast to go!

The first phone in Yakima was in the Yakima Hotel. It was turned on for only part of the day.

Linking the Past to the Present

- What kinds of transportation do you use?
- What is the speed limit on your street? How fast do cars go on freeways?

Activity

My First Ride

Horses pull a car out of the mud. People passing by call out, "Get a horse!"

Study the family in the photo. Pretend you are one of the children, and write a story about what happened that day.

Miners washed ▶ ore to find gold.

This ship stopped in Seattle with a million dollars worth of gold.

GOLD FEVER!

Cities were growing fast. Blocks of tall new buildings filled the downtown areas. Neighborhoods grew up around the city centers. Paved streets replaced the old dirt roads. Stores were full of things to buy.

Seattle was already the state's largest city. Several things helped it grow. One of the most important was the Klondike Gold Rush.

Gold was found along the Klondike River in Alaska and Canada. Another gold rush was on! As news spread, thousands of people headed for the border of Alaska, hoping to strike it rich. Many of them bought food, tools, and warm clothes in Seattle. Then they got on ships headed north. Even the mayor of Seattle left office and went to find gold.

This is how a schoolbook for Seattle children told about the time:

The gold rush began pouring millions of dollars into the city. Stores sold things gold seekers needed. Working day and night, stores tried to keep up with their orders. The sidewalks were piled high with goods.

122

After a long hard trip to Alaska, some men did find gold and got rich in the gold mines. Most, however, spent all their money on supplies and came home poor.

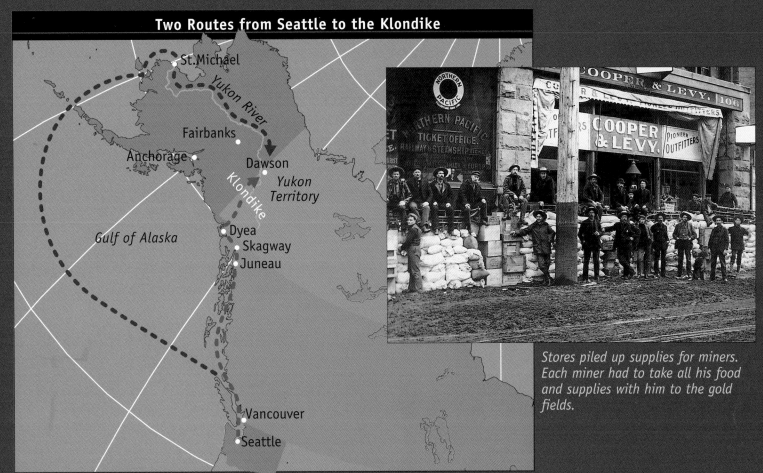

Two Routes from Seattle to the Klondike

St. Michael
Yukon River
Fairbanks
Anchorage
Dawson
Yukon Territory
Klondike
Gulf of Alaska
Dyea
Skagway
Juneau
Vancouver
Seattle

Stores piled up supplies for miners. Each miner had to take all his food and supplies with him to the gold fields.

Dawson was a mining town in the Klondike. Some gold seekers took ships around Alaska and rode on boats down the Yukon River to Dawson. Others took ships to Juneau and then walked over snowy mountain passes to Dawson. Both routes were cold and dangerous.

Lesson 3

Memory Master

1. Why did people want to move to Washington? Give two reasons.

2. Tell two things you learned about the first African Americans in Washington.

3. List two inventions and explain how they made life easier.

4. How did the Klondike Gold Rush help Seattle grow?

Chapter 5 Review

Technology Tie-In

Pick one of the inventions named in this chapter. Do some research to learn about its history. Find at least one way that the invention changed the way people lived.

Geography Tie-In

Use a world map or globe to find the distance between these cities:

- San Francisco, California, to Tacoma by ship
- Canton, China, to Tacoma by ship
- Chicago, Illinois, to Seattle by train
- Dublin, Ireland, to New York by ship and then to Seattle by train

Write a paragraph about the trip you would have liked the best, and why.

Activity

Immigrant Groups

Make a chart like this one on a piece of paper. Fill in the chart to show why each group came, some problems they faced, and how they helped the state grow.

Group	Why They Came	Problems They Faced	How They Helped
European immigrants			
African Americans			
Chinese Workers			

Railroads Bring Change

The railroads made travel easier. The trip across the country could now be done in almost a week. Each train brought things the settlers needed. There were new clothes, new tools, and new furniture. Life was not so hard anymore.

Trains also carried products east to people who would buy them. In this way, people made money.

More people came here to work. This chart shows how fast the cities grew.

City:	Seattle	Tacoma	Spokane
Population in 1880	3,533	1,098	350
Population in 1890	42,837	36,006	19,992

On a piece of paper, number from **1** to **5**, then list all the answers you can find for each question:

1. What changes did railroads bring?
2. Why did people move to Washington State?
3. What happened between 1880 and 1890 that made these towns grow quickly?
4. Which town stayed the largest?
5. Which town stayed the smallest?

For each question, circle the answer you think is most important. Write a sentence to explain your choice.

Activity

Population Chart

Study this chart and answer the following questions:

1. How many years are shown on the graph?
2. Did the population go up or down from 1880 to 1890 ?
3. How many people lived in the state in 1900?
4. What was the population in 1910?

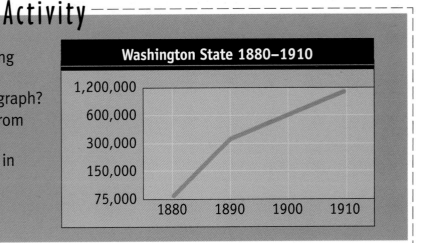

Washington State 1880–1910

THE TIME
1900–1945

"The horseless carriage will never, of course, come into as common use as the bicycle."

—*Literary Digest, 1900*

Beginning the Twentieth Century

Timeline of Events

1900

1899
Mt. Rainier National Park
is established.

1909
Alaska-Yukon-Pacific Exposition

1910

1910
Washington women win
the right to vote.

1914
Panama Canal opens.

1914–1918
World War I

1917
U.S. enters World War I.

19

1919
Seattle General Strike.
Prohibition begins.

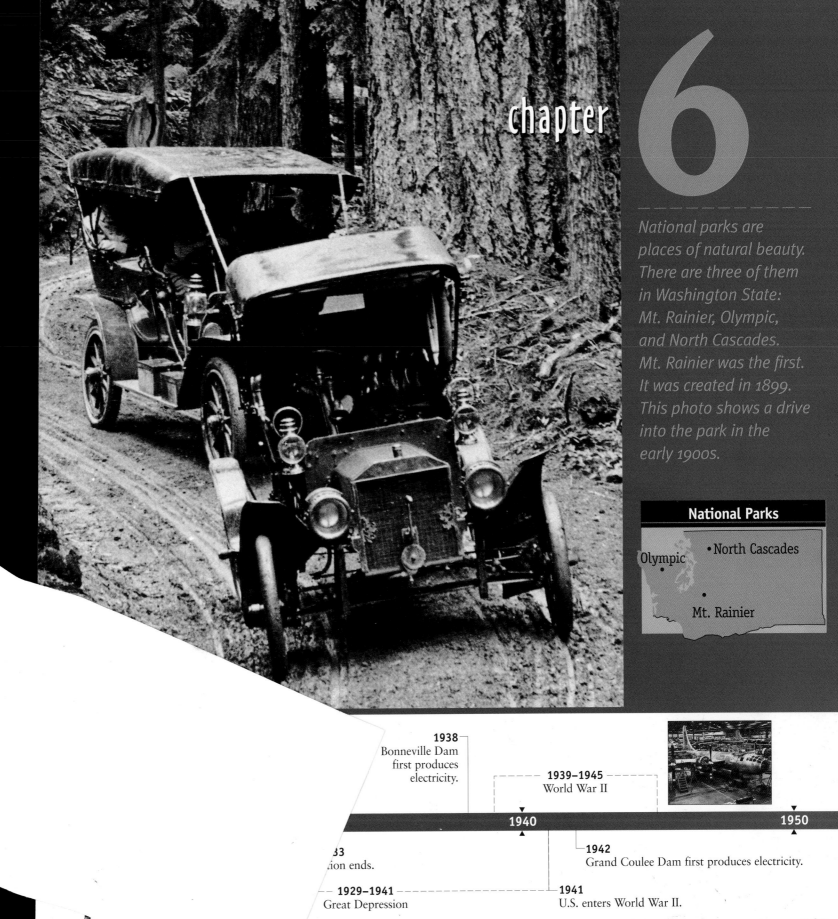

National parks are places of natural beauty. There are three of them in Washington State: Mt. Rainier, Olympic, and North Cascades. Mt. Rainier was the first. It was created in 1899. This photo shows a drive into the park in the early 1900s.

National Parks

Olympic
•North Cascades

•

Mt. Rainier

1938
Bonneville Dam first produces electricity.

1939–1945
World War II

1940

1950

1942
Grand Coulee Dam first produces electricity.

33
ion ends.

1929–1941
Great Depression

1941
U.S. enters World War II.

127

Children at the fair loved the rides. They saw displays of natural resources, too.

SHOWING OFF TO THE WORLD

Washington's people started the new century with pride. Business was booming. The state had the nation's biggest lumber industry. It had the richest wheat farms. The tallest building in the West went up in Seattle.

It seemed like a good time to show the world just how successful the state had become. Seattle leaders suggested a good way to do it. They would put on a fair. They called it the Alaska-Yukon-Pacific Exposition, or the AYP.

For the fair, grand new buildings were put up. They were filled with displays of northwest products and resources. The *forestry* building was a highlight. The room in the center was held up by huge logs. How huge? Each log had enough wood to build five houses!

There was a *carnival,* too, with food, rides, and games. There were special events such as the first cross-country auto race. Thirty cars started in New York. Only five made it all the way to Seattle!

PICTURE POSTCARDS

People wanted their friends in other places to know how much their city was growing. They sent them postcards like these. What postcards can you find in your town today?

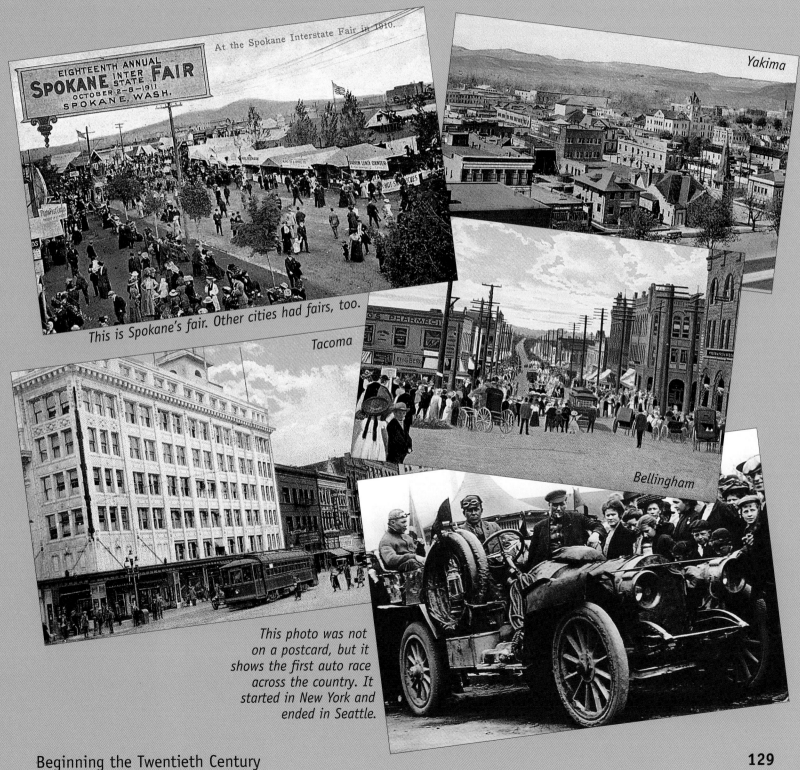

At the Spokane Interstate Fair in 1910.

EIGHTEENTH ANNUAL
SPOKANE INTER STATE FAIR
OCTOBER 2-8-1911
SPOKANE, WASH.

This is Spokane's fair. Other cities had fairs, too.

Yakima

Tacoma

Bellingham

This photo was not on a postcard, but it shows the first auto race across the country. It started in New York and ended in Seattle.

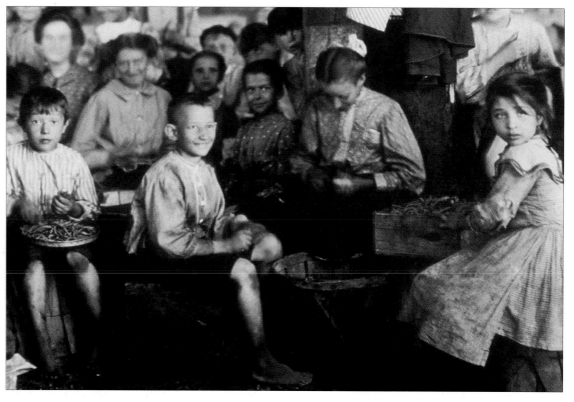

Even children worked in factories and on the farms. Their families needed the money they earned. These children are getting green beans ready to can.

Prohibition

Along with other reforms, many people worked to get the making, buying, or selling of alcohol against the law. They said that drinking alcohol was bad for people. At last, a law was passed to outlaw it. This was called **Prohibition.**

Lawmen dumped out bottles of alcohol if they found them.

WORKING FOR REFORMS

There were a lot of things to be proud of. But many people knew there were also problems to solve.

A lot of the problems had to do with work. Factories, mines, and lumber camps were dangerous places to work. Many people had to work ten or twelve hours a day, six days a week, for low pay. Even children your age sometimes worked this much. Parents had little time for their families. Many children had no time to go to school.

Here and in other places, people worked for *reforms,* or changes in the way things were done. People wanted to be safer at work. They wanted to be able to earn enough money to live on without working so many hours. They wanted safety for workers, especially women and children. They wanted to limit the power of big companies.

Other reforms had to do with government. One of these allowed women to vote. When the United States first became a country, most of the people who could vote were white men who owned land. After the Civil War, black men got the right to vote, too. American women worked hard to win voting rights. It took many years, but the change came at last.

Workers and a boy carry bags and boxes of food home just before Seattle's general strike.

ON STRIKE

Today, many people work eight hours a day, five days a week. But this wasn't always true. Workers used to have to work much longer. They didn't get paid much, either.

One worker alone could not solve these problems. But if all the workers joined together, the owners would have to listen. Loggers did this in 1917. They all stopped working until the boss paid them more and made things better. When all workers stop working, it is called a *strike*. The group they join is called a *union*.

Linking the Past to the Present

Factories, mines, and lumber camps used to be very dangerous places to work. The owners didn't have to make sure workers were safe.

Today, laws make work places safe. Machines have to pass safety tests. Workers might have to wear special clothes or shoes. Ask some adults about safety rules at their jobs.

Seattle's General Strike

Once, a special kind of strike, called a *general strike,* took place in Seattle. This is when *no* workers go to their jobs. It started with a strike in the shipyards. But shipyard workers weren't the only ones having problems. Other unions joined the strike. For five days, workers across the city refused to go to work. Shops were closed. Streetcars didn't run. Only the hospitals stayed open.

In the end, the strike was not successful, but it showed how strong Seattle unions were.

• Seattle

*A **canal** is a waterway made by people. Canals usually connect two rivers or lakes. The Panama Canal is different. It connects two oceans!*

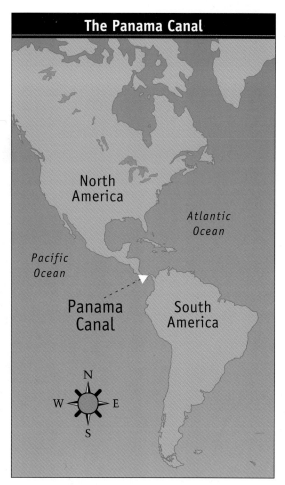

The Panama Canal

North America

Atlantic Ocean

Pacific Ocean

Panama Canal

South America

N
W E
S

Before the canal, what route did ships have to use to travel from one side of North America to the other?

CONNECTED TO THE WORLD

The large fair was a way of showing that our state mattered to the world. Then another event showed how much the world mattered to Washington.

It took place in another country thousands of miles away. A canal was built across Panama. Panama is a narrow country between North and South America. For years, people had thought that if they could dig such a canal, ships could save hundreds of miles of travel. Thousands of men worked for many years to dig the deep, wide waterway though the jungle.

Finally, ships could sail between the Atlantic and Pacific Oceans without having to go all the way around South America. Moving goods back and forth between the Pacific Northwest, the eastern states, and Europe was now much easier.

Lesson 1 — Memory Master

1. What was Washington's first National Park?
2. Name one reason why people in Washington were proud of their state.
3. Name at least one problem people wanted to solve.
4. How did the Panama Canal help our state ship goods to Europe?

The Washington Adventure

WORLD WAR I

One big event made the Panama Canal very important. It was World War I. Almost all countries in Europe fought in the war. Many farms and factories there were destroyed. Many workers became soldiers. The people could not grow the food they needed. They would have to buy it.

Farmers in America got busy. They planted more crops. They bought new machines to help with the harvest. Ships full of Washington vegetables and grain were soon sailing to Europe through the Panama Canal.

The countries at war also needed supplies. They needed everything from guns to bandages. Across America, workers began making these things. There was more work in factories, too. One of these was a new airplane company started by William Boeing. Workers made fifty airplanes for the war.

The United States printed posters to support the war effort.

Loggers and lumber mill workers were also busy during the war. Lumber was used to build ships and homes for all the new workers in the cities.

The biggest boom was in shipbuilding. The navy needed many ships for the war. Before the war, a few hundred people had jobs building ships here. By the war's end, the big *shipyards* in Seattle and Tacoma had more than 50,000 workers! These and other new jobs made the cities grow.

Ships were built to help win the war.

War, Boom Times, and Depression

PEOPLE TO KNOW
William Boeing
Herbert Hoover
Franklin Roosevelt

PLACES TO LOCATE
Europe
Germany
Bonneville Dam
Grand Coulee Dam

WORDS TO UNDERSTAND
Great Depression
New Deal
shipyard
veteran

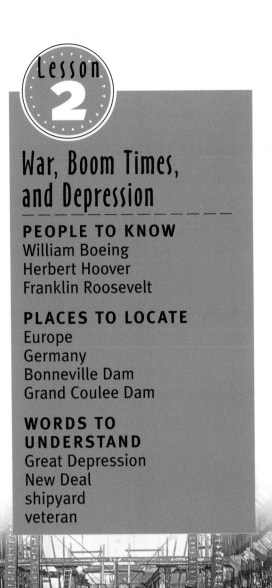

William Boeing

Bill Boeing was a young man when he took his first plane ride. It was just a few years after airplanes were invented, and people didn't know much about them yet. Bill decided he could build a better one.

He and a friend began to work. They hired men to help make a plane and a pilot to fly it. The first one flew pretty well, but they knew they could do better. They kept on planning and testing new ideas.

The Navy was the first buyer, but Bill could see that planes had uses in peacetime as well as in war. Boeing made planes to carry the mail, then he made planes to carry people. Within fifty years, it was the biggest company in Washington.

Boom Times

Three years after the war started in Europe, the United States entered the war. Thousands of workers became soldiers and went to Europe on large ships. There were not enough people left to do all the jobs at home. To get workers, companies promised to pay more than other companies. Wages went up.

The War Ends

Finally, Germany surrendered. The countries agreed to stop fighting. The war was over. At home, soldiers marched through the streets as people cheered.

*The war ended November 11. This day is now Veteran's Day. A **veteran** is a person who served in the armed forces.*

THE ROARING TWENTIES

After the war was over, there were good times across the country. There were plenty of jobs. Americans were making money and buying things. This time was called the Roaring Twenties.

Many families bought their first car during the 1920s. Cars gave people freedom to go wherever they wanted.

People wanted to forget about the war and just have fun. They went to sporting events and cheered for their heroes. Adults went to all-night dance contests to see who could dance the longest. One new dance was the Charleston.

For the first time, women cut their hair short and wore shorter dresses. Men wore black-and-white shoes and wide ties. They cut their hair differently, too.

People started going to the movies. The first movies didn't have sound. A piano player sat next to the screen and played music that was fast or slow to match what was going on in the movie. After a while, movie makers learned how to add sound. Movies with sound were called "talkies."

People who had radios invited their friends to come and listen with them. For the first time, people could listen to voices and music that came from far away. This is an early radio. How is it different from radios today?

Women who wore the new styles and cut their hair short were called "flappers."

The Washington Adventure

HARD TIMES

It seemed as if the Roaring Twenties would go on forever. Then came disaster. In 1929, the nation entered the *Great Depression.* It lasted more than ten years.

A depression is a time when many companies lose business. A lot of people lose their jobs. Because there is no work, most people have little money to spend. Since they can't buy things companies make, the companies don't have jobs for workers.

During the Great Depression, many Americans were out of work. They could not pay for food or clothing. They could not pay their rent. Many had no place to live. Long lines of people waited each day for a bowl of soup to eat. It was the worst depression in our nation's history.

The New Deal

In 1932, the voters elected a new president, Franklin Roosevelt. He had a plan to help end the depression. He called it the *New Deal.*

Part of the plan was to put people back to work. The government would hire workers to build parks, buildings, campgrounds, and roads.

New dams were the biggest projects in the Northwest. Many workers built the dams. Today, the Bonneville Dam helps slow down the fast, rough water of the Columbia River so ships can travel safely. Water stored above the Grand Coulee Dam is used for crops. Both dams make electricity.

These projects gave a big boost to our state. But the depression did not end until the United States entered a new war.

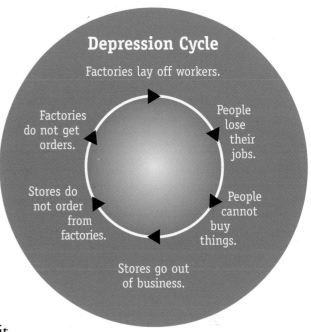

Depression Cycle

Factories lay off workers.

People lose their jobs.

People cannot buy things.

Stores go out of business.

Stores do not order from factories.

Factories do not get orders.

"We ate potatoes three times a day—fried for breakfast, mashed at noon, and in potato salad for dinner. My mother even learned how to make potato fudge."

—*A child during the depression*

What do you think?

Has there been a time when the adults you live with didn't have a way to earn money to pay for a home, food, or other things you needed? What did you do when your shoes got too small or your jeans wore out? How can friends help each other during hard times?

◀ *Many people lost their homes in the Great Depression. Some built shacks of old wood and cardboard. Whole towns of shacks sprang up around the country. They were called "Hoovervilles," after President Herbert Hoover. This one was in Seattle.*

The Big Dam on the Columbia River

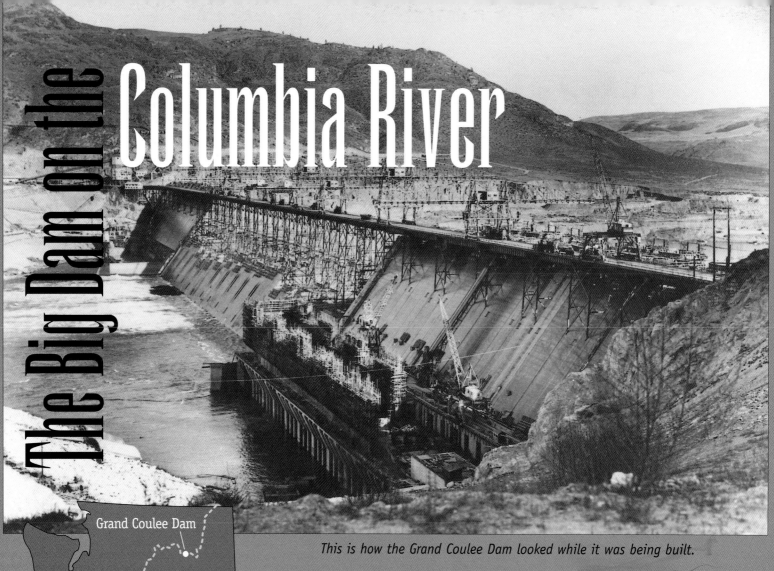

This is how the Grand Coulee Dam looked while it was being built.

Thousands of workers needed a place to live. The town of Grand Coulee sprang up from the desert.

For years, people had talked about building large dams on the Columbia River. They needed a way to use the river water to irrigate their crops. During the Depression, President Roosevelt gave millions of dollars to build two dams. He knew it would provide jobs for men who were out of work.

The dams did more than that. They produced electricity. They helped stop the river from flooding. They provided water for farms and let big ships travel up the river. Dozens of dams were built on the river.

A Big Dam and a New Lake

The biggest dam of all was Grand Coulee. It was a huge project that took many years to build. It is still the largest cement structure in North America. As the river was stopped by the big dam, it backed up. It made a new lake, which was named Lake Roosevelt. Water from the lake is pumped out to farms in the dry part of the state.

Seven thousand men from all over the Pacific Northwest worked on the giant project.

Roll On, Columbia

Not everyone thought making electricity was important. Leaders of the dam project wanted to tell people how important it was. They hired a famous folk singer for one month. His job was to write songs for a film about the dam.

Woody Guthrie wrote "Roll On, Columbia." In 1987, it became Washington's state folk song. Woody Guthrie also wrote another song you might know. He called it "This Land Is Your Land."

Roll On Columbia

Roll on, Columbia
Roll on, Columbia, roll on,
Roll on, Columbia, roll on.
Your power is turning the
* darkness to dawn,*
Roll on, Columbia, roll on.
And far up the river is Grand
* Coulee Dam,*
The mightiest thing ever built
* by man,*
To run the great factories and
* water the land,*
It's roll on, Columbia, roll on.

Photo by Mike Green

At the dam site, a metal sculpture shows Woody singing one of his Columbia River ballads.

Lesson 2

Memory Master

1. Name a business that grew during World War I.
2. Tell some ways that people had fun during the Roaring Twenties.
3. What were some of the things that happened during the Great Depression?
4. How did dams help the people of the Northwest?

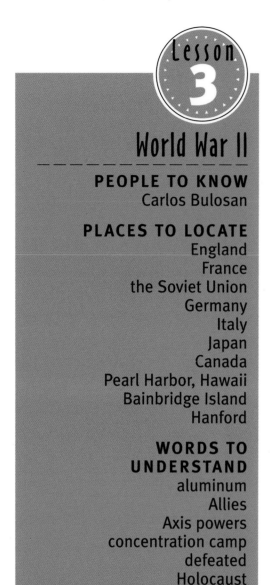

World War II

PEOPLE TO KNOW
Carlos Bulosan

PLACES TO LOCATE
England
France
the Soviet Union
Germany
Italy
Japan
Canada
Pearl Harbor, Hawaii
Bainbridge Island
Hanford

WORDS TO UNDERSTAND
aluminum
Allies
Axis powers
concentration camp
defeated
Holocaust
internment camp
recycle

An ally is a helper, or a friend. Can you see why the countries that helped us in the war were called the Allies?

AT WAR AGAIN

In the 1930s, three countries began to make war against their neighbors. These countries were called the *Axis powers.* They were Germany, Italy, and Japan. Ten years later, many places in the world were under their control.

Then one morning in December, 1941, Japanese planes bombed the U.S. Navy base at Pearl Harbor, Hawaii. The United States entered the war.

Millions of Americans fought in World War II. They joined soldiers from England, France, the Soviet Union, Canada, and other countries. These nations were known as the *Allies.* The Allies fought the Axis powers.

It was a long and terrible war. Millions of people died. The Soviet Union lost the most, with more than 20 million deaths.

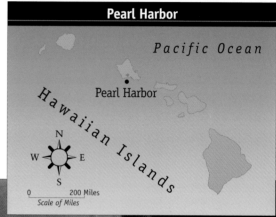

Pearl Harbor

Pacific Ocean

Pearl Harbor

Hawaiian Islands

N
W E
S

0   200 Miles
Scale of Miles

After the Japanese attacked Pearl Harbor, the United States entered World War II.

The Washington Adventure

Navy ships left Washington for World War II battlefields.

The Holocaust

Millions of people who were not soldiers also died during the war. The largest group were Jews. Germany made many laws against Jewish people. They could not run stores and other businesses. They had to wear a star on their clothes.

Jewish families were taken from their homes. They were sent to live in *concentration camps.* These were terrible prison camps. The people were forced to work all day with little food or warm clothes. At night, they slept on wooden slats, stacked high like bunkbeds. More than 6 million Jews were killed.

Finally, Germany and Italy were *defeated,* and the war ended in Europe. Then the United States dropped two bombs on Japan. It was the first time such powerful bombs had been used. It was a very sad time for the people of Japan, but the war was over. The soldiers could come home.

The murder of Jews in Europe is called the *Holocaust*.

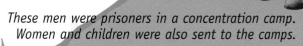

These men were prisoners in a concentration camp. Women and children were also sent to the camps.

Airplanes were the state's most important product during World War II.

WORKING AT HOME

Americans helped the war effort in many ways. Thousands of young men and women joined the armed forces. The army, navy, and air force bases in our state were very busy.

Farms and factories were active, too. They produced food, airplanes, ships, trucks, and other products needed for the war. *Aluminum* is a lightweight metal produced in Washington factories. It was used to make airplanes.

Hanford was a very important center of the war effort. However, almost nobody knew this at the time. It was one of the top-secret places where scientists helped develop the atomic bomb. The project was so secret that most of the workers didn't even know what was going on.

Hanford

New Workers

With so many men away at war, factories needed to find new workers. During the war years, many women worked in factories for the first time. Workers came here from other parts of the country. Many of them were African Americans from other states.

Most of the jobs were in the cities. But workers were also needed on the farms. They were needed the most at harvest time. The United States started a special program to bring farm workers from Mexico. They came each year to pick crops.

Even children helped the war effort. They collected aluminum for *recycling.* Many older children worked at jobs after school.

The Washington Adventure

JAPANESE INTERNMENT CAMPS

Many Japanese Americans had been born in the United States. They were loyal citizens. After the attack at Pearl Harbor, however, many other people grew afraid. They feared that Japanese Americans might help Japan.

The U.S. government gave an order. The Japanese were forced to leave the West Coast. They were sent to live in places called *internment camps.* The Japanese of Bainbridge Island were the first to be sent to the camps.

The camps were in the deserts. Wire fences and guards made the camps like prisons. Families lived in rows of long wooden buildings. The buildings were divided into small rooms. Everyone ate together in one large dining room. The people in the camps started schools for the children. The adults formed clubs and taught each other art, music, and about any subject they could think of. They tried to grow gardens on the dry land.

Many of the people lived in the camps for years. It was a time of sadness and suffering.

My Mom, Pop, and Me

My Mom, Pop, and me
We living three
Dreaded the day
When we rode away,
Away to the land
With lots of sand
My Mom, Pop, and me.

The day of evacuation
We left our little station
Leaving our friends
And my tree that bends,
Away to the land
With lots of sand
My Mom, Pop, and Me

—*Itsuko Taniguchi, 1943*

A Japanese American family moves into the camp.

Filipino Americans

Filipino immigrants worked on Washington's farms. They worked in the fish canneries. But, like other Asian immigrants, they found prejudice here.

Then came World War II. Japanese planes bombed the Philippines on the same day they bombed Pearl Harbor. The Philippines soon came under Japanese control. Later, American and Philippine men fought together to defeat the Japanese. The brave Filipino soldiers won the respect of the Americans.

Carlos Bulosan was a Filipino American poet. He wrote about the hard life and prejudice faced by Filipino farm workers.

What do you think?

If our country were at war with another country today, how should we treat Americans whose ancestors came from that country?

The End of the World War II

World War II changed the lives of many Americans. Millions of people left the towns where they grew up. Black and white soldiers fought side by side for the first time. Women did jobs that women had never done before. People started thinking about themselves and the world in new ways. American culture was changing.

To end the war with Japan, the United States dropped atomic bombs on two cities in Japan. Some of the workers at Hanford had helped make atomic bombs. Luckily, these terrible weapons have never again been used.

Memory Master

Lesson 3

1. Name the two groups who fought each other during World War II.

2. What side did the United States fight on?

3. What was the Holocaust?

4. How did the people at home support the war?

5. What happened to Japanese Americans during the war?

The Washington Adventure

Chapter 6 Review

Geography Tie-In

Since World War II, Americans move around more. Very few children live in the same place where their parents and grandparents grew up.

Find out where your family has lived. Get older family members to help you answer these questions:

1. Where were my grandparents born?
2. Where did they live during their lifetimes?
3. Where were my parents born?
4. Where have they lived?
5. Where have YOU lived?

Make a list of all the places. Beside each place, list the state, country, or continent where it is located. Find all the places on a map.

Activity

Out of Work!

About 25 percent of Washington's people were out of work during the Great Depression. To see what this means, stand up with all of your classmates. Count off from one to four. Then have all the number ones sit down. That's like the number of people who could not get a job during the Great Depression.

Activity

Research World War II

World War II was the most important event of the last century. Learn more about it. Pick one of these topics. Then use library books, an encyclopedia, an atlas, or the Internet to find information about your topic. Write a short report. Share what you learn with the class.

- The war in Europe
- The war in Asia
- China (or another country) during the war
- The Holocaust
- Japanese internment camps
- African Americans during the war
- Women in World War II

THE TIME
1949-2002

"We value the diversity in our society and the con-tributions every culture and group makes. We know we cannot afford to overlook the talents and contributions of anyone because of that person's race, religion, . . . or disability."

—*Governor Gary Locke, 2002*

Timeline of Events

1949 First TV station in Washington. Sea Tac airport opens.

1960s
Civil Rights Movement

1962 Seattle World's Fair

1950   1960   197

1950–1953
Korean War

1964
Civil Rights Act is passed.

1963–1973
Vietnam War

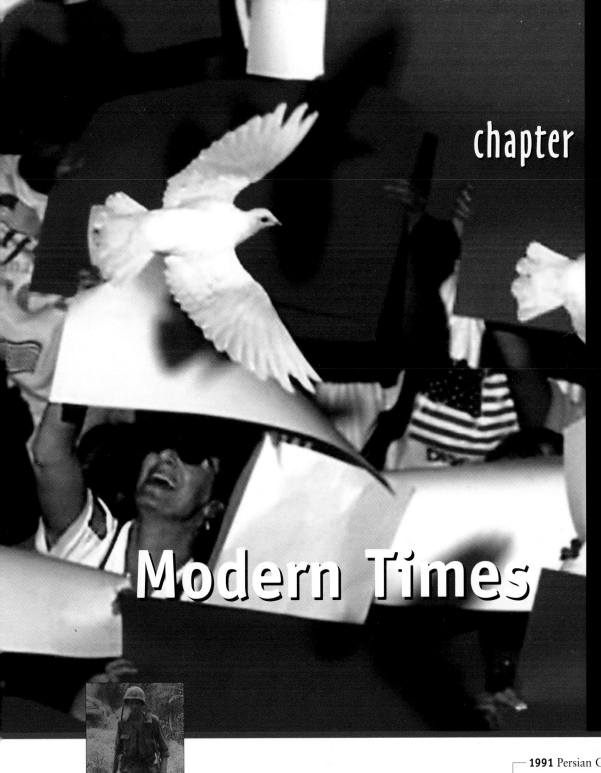

After the terrorist attacks on America, September 11, 2001, over 1,500 people at the Seattle Center raised red, white, and blue paper to form a gigantic American Flag.

Modern Times

1991 Persian Gulf War

2000 A new century begins.

1980	1990	2000

1974 Spokane World's Fair

1991 Cold War ends.

2001
Terrorists attack New York City
and Washington, D.C.

Lesson 1

Growth and Change

PLACES TO LOCATE
Europe
Asia
Samoa

WORDS TO UNDERSTAND
apology
baby boomers
Civil Rights Movement
discrimination
diverse
military
minority group
segregate
suburbs

After World War II, many families moved to new homes outside the cities.

AFTER WORLD WAR II

When World War II ended, the United States was stronger than ever. There were many jobs. Americans were earning more money than ever before.

Like other states, Washington grew. Many people still worked at logging. Other people built airplanes and ships. There were new factories and farms, too. Farmers grew crops they had not planted before, such as potatoes and grapes.

The population kept growing, too. Families felt good about the future and had more children. These children born just after the end of World War II are called *baby boomers.*

The cities grew fast. People moved outside the cities to places called *suburbs.* Some suburbs got so large that they became new cities. Workers drove cars to their jobs in the cities. Many new roads were built. New schools were built for all the children.

There were new ways of shopping, too. The Northgate Shopping Center opened north of Seattle. It was the first shopping center in the nation. People said it was like a small town because it had over 100 shops, a hospital, and a movie theater in one place.

In 1957, children turned on their new black-and-white TV sets to watch Captain Puget *with Bosun Barney the Parrot. All the TV shows were in black and white.*

Linking to the Rest of the World

Other changes helped link Washington cities with the rest of the world. The state's first television station started. People could watch news from other places. People all over the country watched many of the same shows.

The Seattle-Tacoma airport opened a few years after World War II ended. Workers at Boeing built the first passenger jet a few years later. It was called the 707. Work on the state's freeways began about ten years later. It was easier and faster to travel from place to place. Washington no longer seemed so far away from the rest of the nation.

A DIVERSE STATE

Two hundred years ago, groups of Native Americans were the only people here. Ever since then, our state has become more and more diverse. People from many places live here.

Fur traders came from many places. They came from England, Scotland, France, Canada, and Hawaii. Pioneer times brought people from around the United States.

When the railroads were built, more settlers came. They came from Europe and other parts of the United States. Chinese workers came to help build the railroads. Other Asian groups found work here, too.

World War II brought Hispanic and African Americans who came to work here during the war. Many of them stayed.

*A **diverse** place includes people from many places with different cultures.*

__Minority groups__ are those whose race or religion is different from most of the people in the country.

The parents or grandparents of these children came from Taiwan, China, Japan, Mexico, Brazil, Guatemala, Samoa, and Uganda. Can you find these countries on a map?

The Washington Adventure

Hispanic History

Hispanic history in the Northwest goes back a long time. Spanish explorers visited and named the San Juan Islands. They traded furs at Neah Bay. Much later, Spanish-speaking people came to live and work here.

By the 1930s, Hispanic people were living in eastern Washington. Each year at harvest time, more Hispanic workers came to help with the crops. Some of them stayed, and the numbers grew.

Today, people from every Latin American country live and work in our state.

Samoan Immigrants

Samoa is a group of islands in the Pacific Ocean. Many Samoans worked for the U.S. *military* during World War II. Some moved to America when the war was over. A large number settled near the military bases around Puget Sound.

Activity

Alike or Different

We are all different in some ways. We are all alike in many ways. We look different. We live with different people. Some of us like to play soccer. Some of us are good at playing the piano. All of us like to have friends. Most of us would like a pet to play with.

1. Make a list of ten things you need to be happy.

2. Make a list of ten things that all people need to be happy.

What things were on both lists?

Gary Locke
1950–

Growing up in an immigrant family can be hard. Gary Locke knew all about that. His parents were Chinese. The family lived in a busy neighborhood near the center of Seattle.

But Gary Locke was ready to work. He studied hard in class. After school, he worked at his father's store. He kept on working in college and became a lawyer.

In 1982 Locke won his first election and went to Olympia to help make our state's laws. He became a leading lawmaker, but he wanted to do more. He became the head of government for King County. He ran for governor and won. He became the first American of Chinese background ever to hold this job.

THE CIVIL RIGHTS MOVEMENT

All people did not have an equal share of the good life. Minority groups had a hard time getting good jobs. There were other problems, too. Many places, such as hotels, theaters, and restaurants, were *segregated.* There were places where only whites could go.

Many cities were segregated, too. People of different races lived in separate neighborhoods. They went to separate schools.

Many minority people could not even vote. They did not have equal rights. Many people in our state joined with other Americans to try to change this.

African Americans were the first to join together to work for equal rights. In cities around the country, they held big marches. They sat down in the "white only" section of buses and restaurants. They wrote letters and talked to leaders. They wanted new laws to stop discrimination. They wanted to be treated like everyone else.

All these things were part of the *Civil Rights Movement.* Dr. Martin Luther King Jr. was an important leader of the movement. He lived in the South, but he traveled all over the country. He talked to all people about the need for equal rights.

Other Groups Fight for Rights

Other groups faced problems. People of Asian or Hispanic backgrounds still had a hard time getting good jobs. Some were not allowed to vote. Indians were not allowed to catch fish as they always had. All these groups worked for change.

They saw many signs of progress. In Seattle, Asian Americans became city leaders. People of Chinese, Filipino, and Korean backgrounds won city elections. Japanese Americans won an *apology* for the internment camps of World War II. This was a way for the government to say it was sorry for moving the Japanese to the camps. Help was given to Spanish-speaking Americans who wanted to vote. Native Americans won back fishing rights that were promised in their treaties.

Discrimination is when people treat other groups of people badly just because they are different.

DRINK
Coca-Cola

ICE COLD
WHITE CUSTOMERS *Only!*   WHITE CUSTOMERS *Only!*

6¢

◄ *What do you see written on this Coke machine that you would not see today?*

Because of the hard work of these groups, we now have laws to protect our rights. Laws are important, but laws do not always make people think differently. Change is slow. People still work to make sure that all people have equal rights. How can you help?

Women at Work

Minority groups weren't the only people who worked for equal rights. Most jobs that paid well were not open to women. Doctors were nearly always men, and nurses were women. Most bosses were men, while women typed letters and answered the phone. School principals were nearly always men, while most teachers and office workers were women.

In factories and stores, women made less money than men did for the same jobs. Many jobs were not open to women at all.

Women fought for equal pay and equal rights. Our state laws were changed. No longer could Washington make laws that treated men and women differently.

Women worked for equal rights with men.

Memory Master

Lesson 1

1. Name some changes that happened after World War II.

2. What things helped link Washington to the rest of the nation?

3. What things did many people want to change during the Civil Rights movement?

WASHINGTON

PORTRAIT

Carl Maxey
1924–1997

Carl Maxey learned boxing as a boy and became one of the best college boxers in the country. He went on to spend his life fighting for civil rights.

It wasn't an easy life. As a baby, Carl was adopted by a family in Spokane. These parents died when he was just two years old. He was then sent to an orphanage. These were times of prejudice, though. The orphanage would not keep him because he was black. He lived with different families while he grew up.

Carl studied hard. He went to college and then to law school. He became the first black lawyer from the eastern part of our state.

Blacks could not use eating places, hotels, parks, or swimming pools. Maxey worked hard to end discrimination.

This family built a bomb shelter in their basement. They put in beds, blankets, and food in case they had to live in the shelter after an attack. What else do you see in the picture?

Lesson 2

More Wars

PLACES TO LOCATE
Soviet Union
Korea
Vietnam
Cambodia
Persian Gulf
Bosnia
Afghanistan

WORDS TO UNDERSTAND
communist
protest
unpopular
refugee

Seattle school children lie on the floor in the hall for an air raid drill. During the Cold War, people thought that the Soviet Union might bomb their city.

WHAT WAS THE COLD WAR?

The United States and the Soviet Union were allies during World War II. They fought together to defeat Germany. But when the war was over, they became enemies.

Each tried to be the first to explore space. Each tried to be the strongest country. Each tried to win the support of countries around the world. This contest was called the Cold War. It was "cold" because the countries never fought each other with guns.

During the Cold War, people in America were afraid that the Soviet Union might bomb them. Some people built bomb shelters in their basements. School children had bomb drills. They sat under their desks or in the hall until the drill was over.

Both countries built more and more weapons. They wanted to protect themselves in case of an attack.

At that time, the Soviet Union was a ***communist*** country. That means the government owns all the land and businesses and decides what jobs all the people will do. The government also takes care of needs. It provides the people with food, houses, doctors, schools, and so on. The people do not vote for their leaders.

At first, many of the people thought this was a good idea. It seemed like a way to be sure that no one was poor. It turned out to be a terrible failure. In a communist country, people cannot start or own a business. People who work hard are paid the same as people who don't. In the end, the whole country was poor.

The Soviet Union lost the Cold War. The country broke apart.

FIGHTING OVERSEAS

Word War II was the biggest war, but it was not the last. The United States later fought wars in Korea, Vietnam, and the Persian Gulf. Our armed forces also fought in other countries, such as Bosnia and Afghanistan.

Each time, our state's military bases were busy. New members of the armed forces came to the bases to work and to train. Other soldiers and sailors came through on their way home. Our factories were busy, too. They made airplanes and war supplies.

Each war brought new groups of people to live and work in our state. After the Korean War, for example, many U.S. soldiers came home with Korean wives. There were more Korean Americans here than ever before.

A U.S. soldier fights in Vietnam.

A War in Vietnam

The war in Vietnam was the longest in our history. Our soldiers fought in the jungles of Vietnam for more than ten years.

It was also the most *unpopular* war. Many people marched in the streets to *protest* the war. They believed our country was not fighting for a good reason.

The Vietnam War began as a war between North and South Vietnam. The North was a communist country. Our country was against communism, so the United States fought on the side of South Vietnam. The war spread to other countries in Asia.

South Vietnam did not win the war. When it ended, many Asian people there who had worked with Americans no longer felt safe. They left their country. It was a long and hard journey, but many *refugees* finally got to the United States.

Southeast Asia

China

Myanmar

Laos

Thailand

Cambodia

Vietnam

Refugees are people who seek safety, or refuge, in another country.

Lesson 2

Memory Master

1. What was the Cold War?
2. In what other countries did the United States fight wars? Name at least two countries.
3. What was the longest and most unpopular war?
4. Name one way these wars were important to the people of our state.

Many people who worked at Boeing Company lost their jobs and moved out of town. Someone put up this sign as a joke. What does the sign say? What does it mean?

Making a Living

PLACES TO LOCATE
Seattle
Spokane
Puget Sound region
Vancouver, British Columbia

WORDS TO UNDERSTAND
economy
high-tech
research
service

UPS AND DOWNS

The boom times after World War II went on for almost twenty-five years. Then things began to change. The Boeing Company in Seattle lost business. Thousands of airplane workers lost their jobs. Many people left the city. One person put up a large sign on the edge of town. It read, "Will the last person leaving Seattle turn out the lights?"

There were problems in other parts of the state, too. Changes in the lumber industry caused many workers to lose their jobs. Times were hard in logging towns around the state. In some years, the weather was bad, and many farmers lost their crops.

Little by little, things got better. By the late 1980s, the Puget Sound area was growing again. By the 1990s, it was booming! But the way people worked in Washington had changed.

There were fewer jobs in factories. Instead, jobs opened up in *service.* People who serve food, help you get well, fix your teeth, and teach you in school all provide services. More people worked for government, too. More people did *research.*

A New Economy

The *economy* has to do with how people earn and spend money. It has to do with working to make, sell, and buy things. You will learn more about this in the next chapter.

A hundred years ago, our economy was still based on lumber, mining, fishing, and farming. World War II brought a big change. Many more people worked in factories. Airplanes became the state's most valuable product.

By the late 1900s, the economy changed again. Service jobs and high-tech jobs were much more important.

These changes from farms to factories to high-tech business took place across the country. People began to talk about the "old economy" and the "new economy." The old economy made things you could touch, from shoes to ice cream. The new economy is about using and sharing information.

Video games and CDs are part of the new economy. Are there any in your house?

High-Tech Jobs

The fastest growing kind of jobs were the ones we call **high tech.** Making computers, software, and cell phones are all high-tech jobs.

The fastest growing company was Microsoft. It was started in 1975. Twenty years later it was one of the biggest companies in the state. Puget Sound became one of the most important centers of high-tech jobs in the world.

Doctors provide a service when they help you get well. They often use high-tech machines and tools. Research helps doctors learn how to treat sickness.

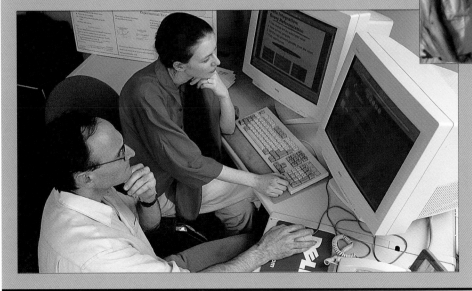

▶ Photo by Kathy Sauber

W🌎rld Fairs

T hree Northwest cities put on world fairs at the end of the century. These fairs were big events. Countries from around the world put up displays in them. Seattle, Spokane, and Vancouver, British Columbia, had large fairs. When they were over, each city had a new place for people to enjoy. Tourists still flock to see the sites of the fairs.

Riverfront Park was the site of Spokane's World Fair. ▼

▲ *The Space Needle was built for the World's Fair in Seattle as a symbol of America's leadership in space. Models of the Space Needle could be seen everywhere. This one was a bird feeder in a family's backyard.*

BEGINNING A NEW CENTURY

As you have seen in this book, our state has had many changes in a short time. It was not such a long time ago that Native American groups were the only people living here. Now our people come from all over the world.

Just 200 years ago, this region was far away from Europe and the eastern United States. Many people did not know about Washington at all. Now, people and products move in and out of Washington from all over the world.

We live in a new century with many challenges. We still need to work hard to:

- protect our environment
- create better transportation systems
- overcome prejudice
- make our schools the best they can be

You will have a chance to make life better in the future. Learning about what people have done in the past is a great way to begin!

Fireworks erupted around the Space Needle ▶
in celebration of the new millennium
that began at midnight on January 1, 2000.

▲▼ Photos by Ben Benschneider/*Seattle Times*

▲ Photo by Greg Vaughn

Memory Master

Lesson 3

1. What happened after almost twenty-five years of boom times following World War II?
2. Name two kinds of business in which many workers lost their jobs.
3. What was the fastest growing company at the end of the last century?
4. Tell some ways our economy changed in the last hundred years.

Chapter 7 Review

Geography Tie-In

1. On a world map, find all the countries in this chapter that were at war.

2. Trace the route that a ship would take to get to each of these countries from the U.S. Navy shipyard in Bremerton.

Activity

The Census—It Counts!

Every ten years, the government has a census. It is a way of seeing who lives in our state and our country. The adults in each house or apartment must fill out a special form. The forms ask questions about how many people live in the house, the ages of the people, and what jobs the adults have.

Census forms also ask people what race they are. Look at the pie graph to see what the census said for the year 2000.

1. How many groups are on the graph?

2. Which is the second largest?

3. If you were a Chinese immigrant, which group would you belong to?

4. If you just moved here from Mexico, what group would you belong to?

5. If your ancestors lived here before explorers and pioneers came, what group would you belong to?

6. The last group says, "Reporting two or more races." What do you think that means?

Group	Percent
White	82.0
Hispanic	7.5
Asian	5.5
African American	3.0
American Indian	1.5
Other	0.5
Reporting two or more races:	3.6

Total Population: 5,894,000

Source: 2000 U.S. Census Report

Activity

September 11, 2001

It was a beautiful morning in Washington State, but soon all Americans watched in disbelief as terrorists took over airplane controls from the pilots and flew airplanes into buildings in New York City and Washington, D.C. Another plane crashed in Pennsylvania. Thousands of Americans were killed. The first war of the twenty-first century began when President George W. Bush and Congress declared war on terrorism.

Far away from New York City and Washington, D.C., the people of the Northwest gathered in parks and churches, along shorelines and streets, and expressed their anger and sorrow. "How could strangers do these terrible things to America?" they asked.

At the Seattle Center, 1,500 people raised red, white, and blue paper to form a huge flag. Then white doves, symbols of peace, were released to fly over the bright flag and into the blue sky.

Do you remember September 11? What do you remember about it? How did you feel?

Make a Poster for Peace

On a colored poster board, add a picture of a flag, people living together in peace, or a symbol of peace. Write about how you feel about peace. Or, write a poem to add to your poster.

At the Seattle Center, 1,500 people raise red, white, and blue paper over their heads to form a gigantic American flag.

chapter 8

*How does Boeing get the
large planes overseas?
Pilots fly them
across the ocean!*

8

For many years, Boeing has been the largest employer in Washington State. Airplanes are made in Washington and sold to many places in the world.

Earning a Living

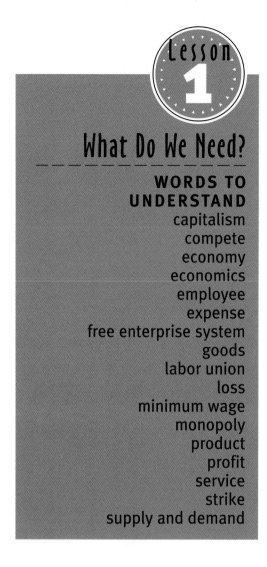

What Do We Need?

WORDS TO UNDERSTAND

capitalism
compete
economy
economics
employee
expense
free enterprise system
goods
labor union
loss
minimum wage
monopoly
product
profit
service
strike
supply and demand

The study of how people get the goods and services they need and want is called *economics*.

Do the adults in your family work at jobs that provide goods, services, or both?

GOODS AND SERVICES

People have needs. They need food, clothing, and shelter. They also have wants. They want things like cars, books, and bicycles. Things workers make for us are called *goods*, or *products*.

People also need care from doctors and nurses. They need education from teachers. They may want help fixing their car. Things workers do for other people are called *services*.

THE FREE ENTERPRISE SYSTEM

An economic system is a way of making, buying, and selling goods and services. There are many different economic systems in the world. The United States has what is called *capitalism* or a *free enterprise system.* Here is how it works:

The people, not the government, own most of the factories and companies that produce goods and services. The owners decide what to produce and how much to charge for it. They decide where to do business. They decide who will help them. They are in charge of selling the product, too.

Building an airplane takes many kinds of workers. Later, when the airplanes are finished, pilots will fly them. The pilots are employees, too.

OWNERS AND EMPLOYEES

Business owners usually hire other people, called *employees*, to work for them. The owner pays the employees for their work.

In a big company such as Boeing, employees do many kinds of jobs. Some design the planes. Some make parts for the planes. Some put the parts together. Other workers sell the planes. The company also has managers, secretaries, and many other kinds of workers.

In a small business, like a hamburger stand or doctor's office, there are few employees. Sometimes the owners and one or two other people do all the jobs.

A good employee must get an education, come to work on time, work hard, and get along with the other workers.

Employees do many kinds of jobs. They earn money for their work. This woman works on the dock, loading goods on ships.

What do you think?

Compare working for someone else with starting your own business. What would you like and dislike about each way of earning money?

Earning a Living

This girl is sorting asparagus.

LABOR UNIONS

Today, it is normal for employees to work eight hours a day, five days a week. But this wasn't always true. Many workers used to have to work much longer. Loggers were an example. They often worked twelve hours a day for little money. Their jobs were also dangerous.

One worker alone could not solve these problems. But if all the workers joined together, the owners would have to listen.

Loggers were one of the many groups of Washington workers to form a *labor union.* Unions protect employees. Union leaders represent the workers. They meet with business owners to discuss pay, safety, and other concerns. If the two sides cannot agree, the employees may decide to go on *strike.* This means they all stop working until the owners give them at least some of what they asked for.

The old logging camps were crowded and uncomfortable. The workers worked from early in the morning until the sun went down. Many men got hurt on the job. They got paid very little. Loggers went on strike to make their jobs better.

Labor unions have played an important role in our history. They helped win an eight-hour workday for all Americans. They helped make workplaces safer.

MAKING A PROFIT

How do business owners make money? Usually they sell what their workers produce. This may be goods or services. An electric company sells electricity. An auto company sells cars and repairs them.

The money a company earns after *expenses* are paid is called a *profit.* For example, a company that makes shoes has to pay for leather, glue, and machines. Workers must be paid for making the shoes. These are expenses. The company must sell the shoes for more than it costs to make them. If not, the owners will have a *loss* instead of a profit. They may soon be out of business.

Supply and Demand

How do business owners decide how much to charge for their products? The selling price depends on a lot of things. One is profit. The price has to be more than the expenses.

The price also depends on how much of the product there is. Sometimes a toy becomes so popular that a company cannot make enough for everyone who wants it. The demand for the toy is higher than the supply. When this happens, the company can sell the toy for a higher price, and people will still buy it. This is called the rule of *supply and demand.*

What happens if the demand goes down, and people don't buy so many toys? The company might sell the toys for a lower price to get people to buy them.

Competition

There are other reasons a company may lower its prices. Suppose there are two companies that make the same toy. They *compete* with each other to sell the most toys. What would happen if one company charged less for its toys? More people would probably buy the cheaper toys.

This is one way that companies compete. There are many other ways. Companies may make new products or better ones. They may offer better services than other companies.

Sometimes there is only one company that produces a certain product. This is called a *monopoly.* The owners can charge whatever price they want. If buyers want that product or service, they will have to pay the price the company charges.

When there is a lot of something, the cost is often lower. If there is not very much of something, the cost is higher.

What do you think?

Is competition good for people who buy things? Why or why not?

Memory Master

Lesson 1

1. What kind of economic system do we have in America? In a few sentences, describe how it works.

2. Tell one way that labor unions help workers.

3. How do business owners decide what to charge for their product? Name at least three things that help them set a price.

4. Tell two ways that government is part of the economy.

Lesson 2

Economics for Everyone

WORDS TO UNDERSTAND

advertising
capital
capital goods
consumer
entrepreneur
factors of production
labor

PRODUCTS AND SERVICES

People are workers. They are also *consumers.* A consumer is a person who buys things. Anyone who spends money is a consumer. Are you a consumer? What kinds of things do you buy with your money?

Most people want to spend their money wisely. They compare different brands to get the best one for their money. They also compare prices at different stores.

Advertising

Because consumers have so many products to choose from, a business tries to sell products by *advertising.* Advertising may be on the radio, on TV, on the Internet, or on signs along the road. Advertising is in newspapers and magazines and may even be in your school. You see and hear it everywhere. Being a wise consumer means understanding how advertising works.

Have you ever bought something because the advertisements made it seem exciting, and then you found out it wasn't? It seemed as if the advertisement lied. Do you believe everything an advertisement says?

Here are some methods used in advertising to get you to buy:

1. **Color and excitement.** The ad is bright and colorful so people will notice it. The product seems fun and exciting.

2. **Repetition.** The ad says a name or slogan over and over so people will remember it.

3. **Social appeal.** The ad suggests that if you use a certain product you will look nice and have a lot of friends.

4. **Humor.** People like and remember things that are funny.

5. **Music.** People remember short tunes and jingles.

Does this ad for Wild Things sunglasses ▶
make you want to buy a pair?

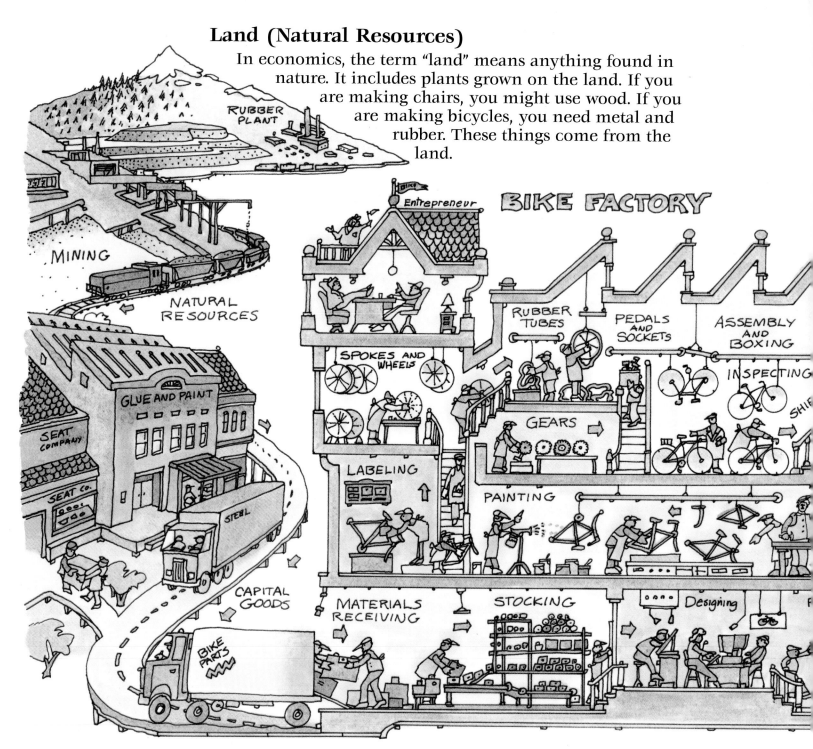

Land (Natural Resources)

In economics, the term "land" means anything found in nature. It includes plants grown on the land. If you are making chairs, you might use wood. If you are making bicycles, you need metal and rubber. These things come from the land.

Capital Goods

When you use things that are already made to make something else, you are using capital goods. A carpenter doesn't make his own hammer—he or she just uses it to build a house. The hammer and nails a carpenter uses are capital goods. The money you need to start and run a business is also called capital.

Labor

Labor is the work that people do. Carpenters, teachers, sales people, lawyers, secretaries, actors, race car drivers, and basketball players all do labor. The workers in a bicycle factory are doing labor. That is how they make money.

Factors of Production

There are four things that must come together before something is sold as a good or service. These things are called factors of production. Factors of production are land, capital goods, labor, and entrepreneurs.

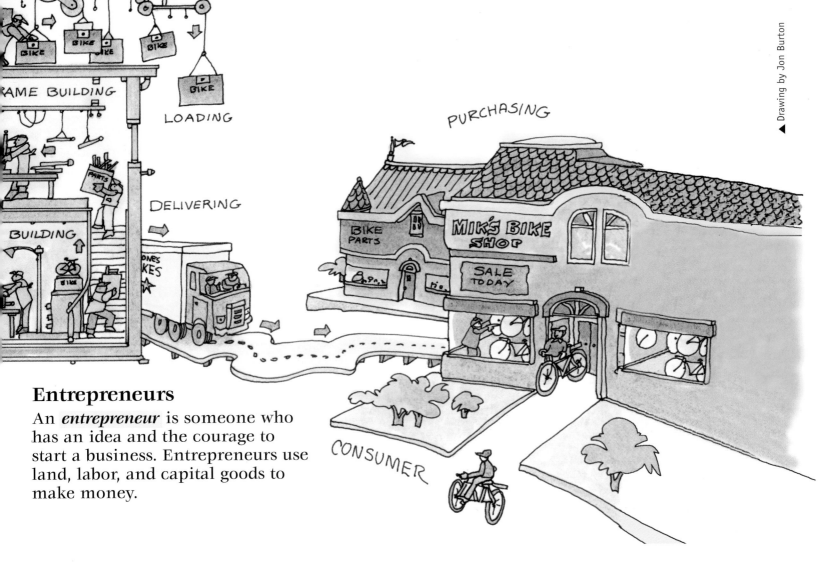

▲ Drawing by Jon Burton

Entrepreneurs

An *entrepreneur* is someone who has an idea and the courage to start a business. Entrepreneurs use land, labor, and capital goods to make money.

WASHINGTON ENTREPRENEUR$

Think about the early settlers and pioneers. A lot of them came here hoping to earn a living by farming, but many came to work in other businesses. They even started their own businesses. Here are a few examples from our history:

Ben Snipes

As a teenager, Ben Snipes worked on a pack train that carried apples to gold miners in California. Then, when gold was discovered in British Columbia in 1859, Snipes hurried north. Again, he saw the chance to sell food to miners. He began buying cattle so he could sell the beef.

When the mining slowed down, Snipes found new places to sell his products. Soon he had thousands of cattle grazing the grasslands of eastern Washington. Each spring, his cowboys rounded up the herds and walked them south to the new railroad. Trains carried his cattle to markets around the country. For a short time, eastern Washington was cowboy country and Ben Snipes was "cattle king."

Chin Gee Hee

Chin Gee Hee was the best-known Chinese settler in Washington Territory. His first business was a laundry in Port Gamble. He later went to work for the railroad. After a while, he found a new job hiring railroad workers. He hired many Chinese men. He settled in Seattle and became a well-known businessman. He built the first building after the Seattle fire. Chin Gee Hee returned to China a rich man.

Pack trains carried supplies and food to miners.

Chin Gee Hee

172

Thea Foss

The Foss family moved from Norway to Tacoma in 1888 and lived in a little house by the water. Andrew Foss could not always find work, so Thea began to rent rowboats from their home. The Foss family's boat business grew. Today, you can see Foss tugboats all around Puget Sound.

Thea Foss

Eddie Bauer

Eddie Bauer began selling sporting goods in Seattle in the 1920s. At first, he sold mostly tennis and golf equipment, but his business really grew when he began including products for fishermen and hunters.

Later, Bauer sold outdoor clothing, opened other stores, and became a national success.

Eddie Bauer

Bill Gates and Paul Allen

Washington's most famous modern entrepreneurs are Bill Gates and Paul Allen. They became interested in computers when they were high school students in Seattle. At that time, computers were as large as a room. But these boys believed that change was coming. Soon, computers will be everywhere, they said. In 1975, they started the company called Microsoft. Today, it is the largest computer software company in the world.

Bill Gates

Memory Master

Lesson 2

1. Name three ways advertising attracts customers.
2. What are the four factors of production?
3. Name an entrepreneur and tell what business he or she started.

Activity

Young Entrepreneurs

Adults are not the only people who become entrepreneurs. Children can, too. What business could you start? Will you provide goods or a service? Choose something you like. That is very important. You are more likely to stay with something you enjoy.

After you pick your business, make a list of all the things you will need. Decide if each thing is an example of land, labor, or capital goods.

Here are some ideas to help get you started.

Service Suggestions:

- **House Watcher**
  While people are away on vacation, offer to get their mail, turn on lights, and water their plants.

- **Dog Walker**
  Many people with dogs don't get home from work until late. Offer to walk their dogs for them after school and on weekends.

- **Garbage Can Service**
  Offer to take cans out to the street on collection day and put them back where they were after school.

Canning and selling salmon became a big business. Many of the early cannery workers were Chinese.

Lesson 3

Earning a Living Today

WORDS TO UNDERSTAND

agriculture
export
interstate
high-tech
military
scientific
tourist
tourism
trading partners

ECONOMICS IN EARLY TIMES

Today, all Americans use the capitalist, or free enterprise system. However, this kind of system did not always exist here.

American Indians had a different economic system. They believed that no one had the right to own the land. Different tribes lived in different regions of the land. All the people in the tribe shared the land and its resources. People hunted and fished together to provide food for all the members of the group. They also traded fish and other things with other groups.

When fur traders came to the Pacific Northwest, things began to change. The traders killed too many wild animals and took the furs to sell. Within a short time, there were few sea otters or beavers left.

As settlers arrived, the economy changed quickly. People claimed land and put up fences. They raised crops and cut down trees to sell. Soon trading ships were carrying Northwest products across the ocean and bringing in new products for people to buy.

The Washington Adventure

People no longer met all their needs themselves. Instead, they bought and sold goods and services. Stores and businesses opened around the Northwest.

Money

Native Americans traded for goods and services. A woman who wove beautiful baskets might trade a basket for something she needed, such as food. Settlers also traded what they had for tools, shoes, and cloth.

This worked well sometimes, but not always. Suppose a family needed shoes, but the shoemaker didn't need the farmer's eggs. Trading wouldn't help the family meet its needs.

A system of money solved this problem. A family could sell their eggs to one person and use the money to buy goods from another person.

Today, money is printed by the federal government. It's one way that government is important to our economic system.

MAKING A LIVING TODAY

When Washington became a state, our economy was based on natural resources. Logging was the most important business. Fishing, farming, and mining were also important. Towns grew up near farms, forests, or mines. There were jobs in sawmills, food-packing plants, or other businesses that used natural resources.

During the twentieth century, fishing, farming, and mining slowly became less important. As this happened, there were fewer jobs in small towns. Many people moved to big cities.

In the cities, shipbuilding and then airplane manufacturing were the largest businesses in our state. Today, manufacturing still provides many jobs. However, the new *high-tech* economy is becoming more and more important. Computer software and medicines are some of the important new products.

There are many other kinds of work in the cities. Seattle and the Tri-Cities are important centers of *scientific* research. In Bremerton, Everett, Spokane, and the Tacoma area, the *military* is an important employer.

Businesses that provide services, such as restaurants and hospitals, provide a large number of jobs around the state. Many people also work for the government.

Many children save money to help pay for something they want. Do you save money?

Saving and Planning

Money gives us a way to plan ahead for things we will want later. Suppose you get an allowance from your family or start a business. You might walk dogs or mow lawns. Suppose you earn $10 each week and you want to buy a bicycle that costs $150.

You could save your money until you have enough for the bike. How long would it take if you saved all of the $10 each week? How long would it take if you saved $5 and spent $5?

You could save your money in a bank. Banks are businesses that help people manage their money. They are safe places to keep savings. They also make loans. People can go to a bank to borrow money to buy a house or car.

TRADING AROUND THE PACIFIC RIM

Many people work in world trade. World trade includes all the jobs involved in buying and selling things to other countries.

Our most important *trading partners* are the countries of the Pacific Rim. Each country around the Pacific Rim makes products that people in other countries want to buy. For example, we can buy cars made in Japan or toys made in China. People in these countries buy airplanes, software, and other products made here.

Transportation by Land, Air, and Sea

Transportation of natural resources and finished products is very important for business. Without good transportation, business would almost stop.

Today, most products are shipped in containers. These big metal boxes can be loaded onto a ship, train, or truck. You can see containers on three important forms of transportation:

- **Waterways:** Puget Sound is our most important waterway. Seattle and Tacoma are our busiest ports. Ships and barges also travel on the Columbia and Snake Rivers.

- **Railroads:** Railroads were important in our history, and they are important to our economy today. Trains carry Pacific Rim products to cities around America.

- **Roads and highways:** Two major highways cross Washington State. I-5 runs north and south near Puget Sound. I-90 crosses the state from Seattle to Spokane. The "I" stands for *interstate.* These big roads cross many states. Smaller roads and highways connect our towns, cities, and neighborhoods.

There is one other main form of transportation in Washington. Can you guess what it is? If you guessed airplanes, you're right. Sea-Tac is the largest airport in the state. There are smaller airports in Spokane and other cities.

High-tech equipment is an important export.

What We Make and Sell

The word **export** means things we send OUT of the state or the country.

Washington's Top Exports (in order of total sales)

- airplanes
- computer software
- farm products, including apples, wheat, cattle, and dairy products
- electronic and scientific equipment
- wood products
- machinery
- medical equipment
- medicines

Trains carry containers of Washington products to the shipping ports.

Earning a Living

APPLES, WHEAT, AND MORE

Most people live in cities, but agriculture is still big business in Washington. Our state is the nation's largest producer of apples, cherries, pears, asparagus, and several other crops. Apples are our most valuable farm product, followed by wheat and potatoes. Washington is also an important ranching state. Cattle are raised and sent to market for beef.

These photos show some important farm products. Can you name them?

Agriculture is raising plants and animals to sell for food. Do you know anyone who has a job in agriculture?

In the Skagit Valley, miles of tulips are grown for their bulbs. When people buy the bulbs and plant them in their yards, the beautiful tulips will bloom again the next spring. ▼

▲ Photo by Dwight Morgan

▲ Hay is grown to feed cattle and other animals.

The Washington Adventure

These boys have come to hike the trails of ▶
Mt. Rainier National Park. Can you read their
T-shirts? What other places have they visited?

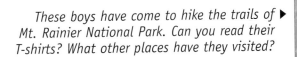

People come to enjoy our many rivers and lakes. Have you ever been in a kayak?

ENJOY WASHINGTON!

Each year, thousands of people visit here from other states and countries. They come to hike and ski in our mountains, sail on our waters, visit our parks, and enjoy our cities. While here, they stay in hotels, eat at restaurants, and attend a local fair, festival, or rodeo.

All the things that *tourists* do in our state make money for our businesses and workers. They are all part of a major industry in our state called *tourism*.

Tourists often visit our cities. This historic home is in Port Townsend.

Earning a Living

THE WASHINGTON ECONOMIC ADVENTURE!

Making a book is an adventure! It is part of the economics of Washington and other places in the world.

This book is a good example of how free enterprise works. An entrepreneur started a book publishing company. The owner of the company and his employees wanted to make a book that children and teachers would really like. They also hoped the principal would like the book enough to buy it, so the company could make a profit. It took the services and products of many people in different parts of the world to make the book. Here is what happened:

The author in Washington studied Washington's history. She went to libraries and read books about the state. She read the diaries of people who had lived here a long time ago. The author wrote the words and typed them on a computer. She worked hard to make the book interesting and tell a true story of Washington. She gathered many photographs.

The editor in Utah made sure the spelling and writing were right. An artist in Utah drew some of the pictures. A different artist used a computer to place the words and pictures on each page. All of these things took over a year to do.

When the book was ready to be printed, it was sent across the Pacific Ocean. The paper came from trees in Asia. Someone made and sold the ink to the printer. Many workers in Asia used huge presses to print the book. They used machines to sew the pages together and glue the covers on.

After about four months in Asia, the books were brought to America on a ship. The ship landed in California. Then trucks brought large boxes of books to Washington.

All of the people who worked on the book had to be paid for their services. All of the machines, computers, and even ink had to be paid for. Where did the money come from?

You and your friends are the consumers. Your school paid for your books. If your school is a public school, it got the money from the local government. The government got the money from taxes. The taxes were paid by the adults in your town or county. If your school is a private or parochial school, part of your fees helped to pay for the books. Adults earned the money from their jobs or businesses to pay their taxes or your fees.

So there you have it! People work hard to provide the goods and services other people need. The work makes them feel good about themselves. It provides money for the workers and their families. The work helps provide for the needs of everyone.

Memory Master

Lesson 3

1. Tell three ways that the early American Indian economic system was different from ours today.
2. What businesses were most important when Washington became a state?
3. What businesses are most important in the state today? (Name at least four.)
4. Name three agricultural products of Washington.
5. Name four forms of transportation in the state today.

Chapter 8 Review

Activity

If I Had a Job

Someday you will be an adult and work at a job. If you could choose any job in the world, what would it be? In what part of the economy would your job be—farming, manufacturing, service, or something else? Do you know how much money a week you will make at the job? What kind of training will you need?

Make a poster that shows you working at the job. Write a few sentences about what you are doing at your job.

Geography Tie-In

Give examples of two businesses for each word on the list below. You can use this chapter and the businesses in the yellow pages of a phone book to help you.

- natural resources
- manufacturing
- agriculture
- service
- high tech
- tourism
- transportation

Which of these businesses depend on Washington's geographic features such as location, climate, land, and resources? Which do not?

Technology Tie-In

In this chapter, you learned a little about high-tech jobs. Do some research. Ask an adult to help you look in library books, an encyclopedia, a dictionary, and on the Internet to learn more about the many kinds of high-tech jobs.

Tell as much as you can about one of the jobs.

Would you like to work in a high-tech job when you get older?

Goods and Services

Goods are things that people produce. Goods may be made in factories, farms, workshops, or even at home. They are then sold for money. Shoes, pencils, televisions, and dog collars are all goods. People make money by making and selling goods.

Services are things that people do for other people. Dentists, sales clerks, umpires, coaches, and your teacher provide services. People earn money by providing services.

Don't be fooled! Many people who provide a service also sell goods. The sales clerk, for example, is providing a service by selling shoes. The shoes are goods, but the sales clerk provides a service by selling them to you.

On a separate piece of paper, number from one to fifteen. Write **G** for goods or **S** for services for each job listed below.

1. Makes books
2. Fixes your teeth
3. Teaches students
4. Manufactures paint
5. Paints pictures to sell
6. Makes engines for cars
7. Repairs cars
8. Makes cheese
9. Delivers cheese to grocery stores
10. Makes telephones
11. Repairs telephones

The World in Your Closet

You are an important part of the world economy. Really! You and your family use things that are a part of world trade. Look around your house to see if you can find things that were made in other countries.

1. Search your closet and drawers. Read the labels on your clothes. Where were your clothes made?

2. Examine your kitchen cupboards and refrigerator. Look for labels on cans and packages. Where was the food grown or packaged?

3. Ask adults you know where their cars were made. How do you think the cars got to your house?

chapter 9

THE TIME
1775–Present

Every person may freely speak, write and publish on all subjects, being responsible for the abuse of that right.

Washington State Constitution
(Article 1, Section 5)

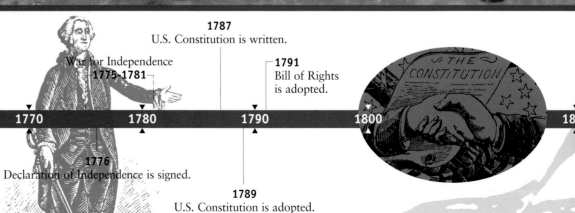

Timeline of Events

1787
U.S. Constitution is written.

War for Independence
1775–1781

1791
Bill of Rights is adopted.

THE CONSTITUTION

| 1770 | 1780 | 1790 | 1800 | 18 |

1776
Declaration of Independence is signed.

1789
U.S. Constitution is adopted.

9

The Fourth of July was the most important holiday of the year throughout the Northwest. People had parades like this one in Davenport about a hundred years ago. What famous event do we celebrate on the Fourth of July? How did that event affect our country?

Government for All of Us

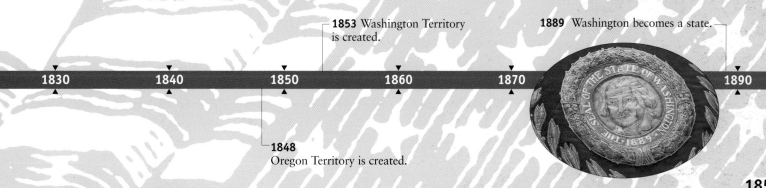

1853 Washington Territory is created.

1889 Washington becomes a state.

| 1830 | 1840 | 1850 | 1860 | 1870 | 1890 |

1848
Oregon Territory is created.

An Independent Country

WORDS TO UNDERSTAND

capital
citizen
colonies
compromise
Congress
constitution
dictator
document
elect
federal government
local
representative

The Thirteen Colonies

Philadelphia

This map shows the thirteen colonies that became the first thirteen states.

A colony is a settlement under the rule of another country far away.

AN IMPORTANT YEAR

In our country, 1776 was an important year. It was the year the American *colonies* signed the Declaration of Independence in Philadelphia. This is one of the most important *documents* in American history. It was written with pen and ink on large paper. It tells why the people wanted to rule themselves. It states some of the most important ideas of our government.

Study this quote from the Declaration of Independence. The words seem old-fashioned now, but the ideas do not.

The Words:

We hold these truths to be self-evident: that all men are created equal, that they are endowed by their Creator with certain . . . rights, that among these are Life, Liberty, and the pursuit of Happiness. That to secure these rights, governments are instituted among Men, deriving their just powers from the consent of the governed.

The Ideas:

- All people are equal.
- All people were born with basic rights.
- Governments exist to protect these rights.
- Governments are given powers by the people.

THE WAR FOR INDEPENDENCE

Have you ever been outside when suddenly the sky turned dark, and before you knew it, the sound of thunder was in your ears? That is how the American Revolution started in the thirteen colonies.

England did not want to lose its colonies in America. It sent soldiers in ships across the Atlantic Ocean to fight the Americans. The colonies had to fight a war to win their independence.

George Washington was the leader of the American soldiers. They fought a long war. Men on both sides were killed. The Americans finally won the war. The United States of America was a free country.

WE HOLD THESE TRUTHS TO BE SELF-EVIDENT: THAT ALL MEN ARE CREATED EQUAL, THAT THEY ARE ENDOWED BY THEIR CREATOR WITH CERTAIN INALIENABLE RIGHTS, AMONG THESE ARE LIFE, LIBERTY AND THE PURSUIT OF HAPPINESS, THAT TO SECURE THESE RIGHTS GOVERNMENTS ARE INSTITUTED AMONG MEN. WE... SOLEMNLY PUBLISH AND DECLARE, THAT THESE COLONIES ARE AND OF RIGHT OUGHT TO BE FREE AND INDEPENDENT STATES...AND FOR THE SUPPORT OF THIS DECLARATION, WITH A FIRM RELIANCE ON THE PROTECTION OF DIVINE PROVIDENCE, WE MUTUALLY PLEDGE OUR LIVES, OUR FORTUNES AND OUR SACRED HONOUR.

The words of the Declaration of Independence are engraved in stone on a wall of the Jefferson Memorial in our nation's capital.

Who is the man standing up, talking about ideas for the new Constitution? He was chosen to be the first president of our country. Our state was also named after him.

Today, *citizens* of the United States include all people who are born here and those who have passed a special test to become citizens.

GOVERNMENT FOR A NEW NATION

After the United States became a country, Americans had an important task. They had to create a government for their new country. They did not want a king or queen, as England had. They wanted a way to rule themselves.

Leaders from each state met in Philadelphia, Pennsylvania. For many days, they talked about what kind of government the United States should have. They wrote our ***Constitution.*** A constitution is a set of basic rules and ideas for government. Here are a few of the most important ideas of the United States Constitution:

- Government of the people
- Rule of law
- Limited power
- Levels of government
- Three branches balance the power of government

Let's learn more about each of these ideas:

Government of the People

Citizens have the right to choose their government leaders. We do this by voting. If voters do not like what their leaders are doing, they can ***elect*** new leaders the next time they vote. In this way, the government gets its power from the people.

The Washington Adventure

Rule of Law

The Constitution says what the government can and cannot do. Government leaders make the laws. They must obey the laws and the Constitution. This is called the **rule of law.** It is different from a government headed by a king or a *dictator* who can rule however he wants to.

Limited Power

The Constitution limits the power of the United States government in several ways. For example, much power is saved for the states. The people in one part of the country can make laws that are different from the laws in another part. The states give some of their power to counties and cities. Power is shared by these three **levels of government.**

Levels of Government

We all live under three levels of government. *Local* is close to home. State government is for the whole state. National government is also called the *federal government.* It is government for the whole United States.

Each level has different jobs, as this chart shows.

Democracy: rule by the majority (more than half the voters)

Republic: the people elect representatives to make the laws

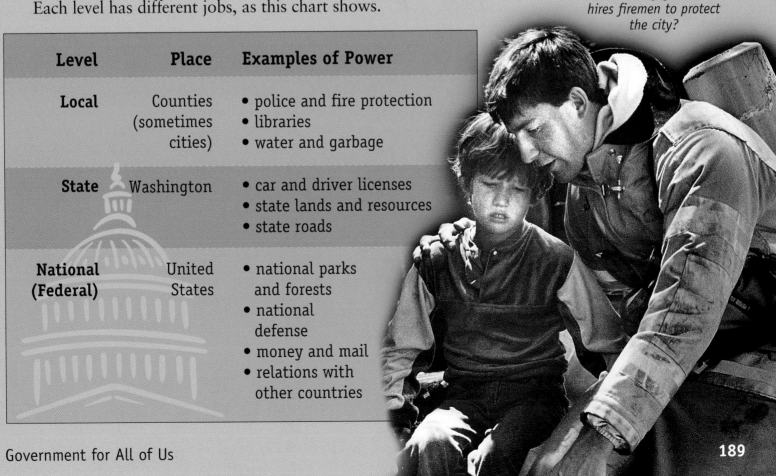

Which level of government hires firemen to protect the city?

Level	Place	Examples of Power
Local	Counties (sometimes cities)	• police and fire protection • libraries • water and garbage
State	Washington	• car and driver licenses • state lands and resources • state roads
National (Federal)	United States	• national parks and forests • national defense • money and mail • relations with other countries

Government for All of Us

Three Branches and Balance of Power

Power is also shared by three main parts, or **branches of government:**

- The **legislative branch** makes laws.
- The **executive branch** carries out laws.
- The **judicial branch** decides what laws mean.

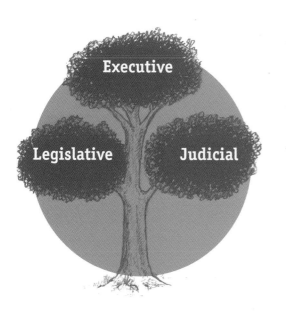

A New Park

What if people are thinking about making a new park? The legislative branch—the lawmakers—study the idea. Then they vote. If they vote yes, they approve the money to build a new park.

Then the executive branch takes over. This branch will carry out the law. People who work for that branch will buy the land, plan the park, and see that it is built.

Now, what if there is a problem? What if the law is not clear about what can and cannot be done in the park? This is where the judicial branch comes in. It is the branch that includes our courts and judges. The judge would study the laws, listen to both sides, and decide what should be done. The courts would also get involved if someone broke a law inside the park.

Activity

Research Levels of Government

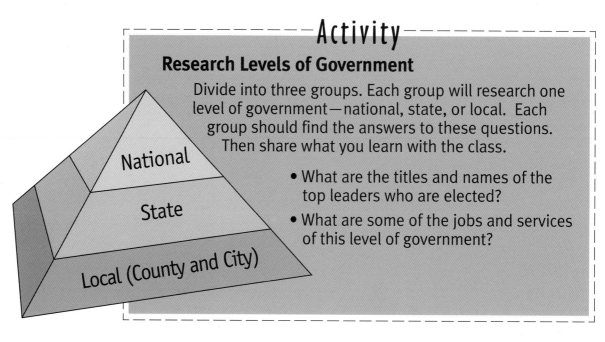

Divide into three groups. Each group will research one level of government—national, state, or local. Each group should find the answers to these questions. Then share what you learn with the class.

- What are the titles and names of the top leaders who are elected?
- What are some of the jobs and services of this level of government?

EQUAL REPRESENTATION

The writers of the Constitution faced a hard problem. Some people wanted each state to have an equal number of representatives to make the laws for the country. But the big states thought this was unfair. A larger state should have a larger number of lawmakers, they said.

The writers decided on a *compromise.* That is when both sides have to give up part of what they want so a decision can be made.

The writers decided that the legislative branch, called *Congress,* would have two parts, the **Senate** and the **House of Representatives.** Both parts would make the laws.

Each state would have two **senators** to make laws in the Senate. But bigger states would have more **representatives** than smaller states. This was a way to make sure that people in all parts of the country have an equal say in government.

Representatives in Congress

Representatives from Washington State and each of the fifty states go to Washington, D.C. to make laws for the whole country. Our two United States senators are elected by all the voters in the state.

Washington also has nine members of the House of Representatives. Each represents a different part of the state.

In the early colonies and in pioneer times, people often talked and then decided by themselves what to do. Today, we elect *representatives* to make our laws.

Our State's Representatives to Washington, D.C.

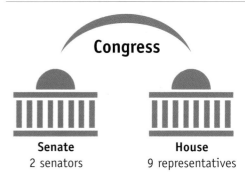

Congress

Senate
2 senators

House
9 representatives

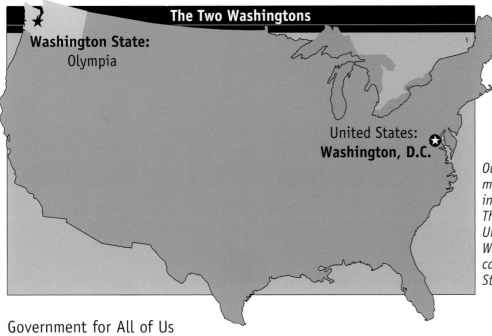

The Two Washingtons

Washington State:
Olympia

United States:
Washington, D.C.

*Our representatives meet and make laws in the **capital** cities. The capital of the United States is Washington, D.C. The capital of Washington State is Olympia.*

What do you think ?

Why is it good to have a representative from each part of the state? Do the people who live near you have different interests than people in other parts of the state?

Activity

Your Representatives

Who are your senators and representatives to the federal government? Is there something important that you would like them to do for Washington or the nation?

Discuss this with your class and write a letter to them. You can get their names and addresses in a telephone book under Government, or from this website: **www.congress.org**

Memory Master

Lesson 1

1. What is the Declaration of Independence?

2. What is a constitution?

3. Pick one of these important ideas of our country's Constitution and tell what it means:
    • Government of the people
    • Rule of law

4. Name the three levels of government.

5. Name the three branches of government and tell what each one does.

6. Name the two parts of Congress.

The Washington Adventure

THE BILL OF RIGHTS

Many people believed that one important thing was missing from the U.S. Constitution. They wanted a clear list of the rights belonging to all Americans. They wanted to be sure that the government could never take away these rights. Ten changes, or *amendments,* were later added to the Constitution. They are called the Bill of Rights.

Here are some of these rights:

- Freedom of religion: You can choose what to believe. You may join any religion or none at all.

- Freedom of speech: You are free to talk about your ideas. You can share your ideas with government leaders.

- Freedom of the press: People may print their opinions in books, newspapers, and in other ways.

- Freedom of assembly: People can meet peacefully together.

- Equal justice: Anyone accused of a crime will receive fair and equal treatment. Punishment will not be cruel.

- Safety: The government cannot break into your house and take things. You can keep a gun in your home. You cannot be forced to keep soldiers in your home.

What do you think?

Does freedom of speech mean you can write *graffiti* on public property? Can you say false things that bring harm to others? How can we use our freedoms so they don't hurt others?

CITIZEN RESPONSIBILITIES

Along with each of our rights come *responsibilities.* We all need to respect the rights of others. We must all obey the laws that our elected leaders have made.

Adults have a responsibility to take part in their government. This is what "government of the people" is all about. The main way to do this is by voting.

There are many other things that all people can do. The first step is to learn how government works. You're doing that right now! You can talk with your parents about rules and laws and why they are important to your family.

Rights and Responsibilities

WORDS TO UNDERSTAND
amendment
graffiti
responsibility

Freedom of assembly means that you are free to meet with other people. You can do this anytime you want, as long as the meetings are peaceful.

Freedom of the press means you can write or print anything that you think is important.

Being a Good Citizen

Being a good citizen means helping make sure your town, state, and nation are good places to live. Here are a few ways you can do this. What others can you think of? Discuss these ideas as a class and make a list on the board.

- Obey the laws and respect the rights of others.
- Take care of the environment. Recycle. Don't litter. Don't pollute.
- Join a group that helps make your city a better place to live.
- Share your opinions with government leaders through letters, calls, e-mail, or visits.
- Keep learning more about government and how it is important to your city or town.

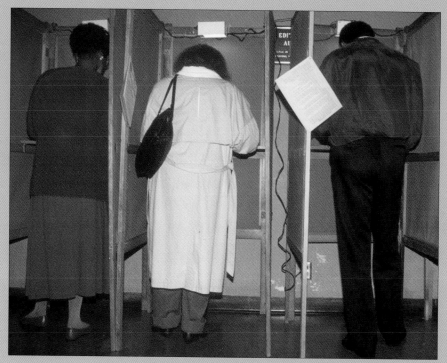

Voting is done secretly in a voting booth.

What do you think?

Every American citizen age eighteen and over can vote. Do you think voters should be older or younger than this? At what age do you think YOU will be ready to help choose our leaders?

Lesson 2

Memory Master

1. What is the Bill of Rights?
2. List at least four kinds of freedom that all Americans have.
3. Name at least three things all good citizens should do.

STATE CONSTITUTION AND LAWS

The people in each state have to live by the Constitution and the laws of the federal government. Each state also has its own constitution and its own government.

The state governments make laws that have to do with the land and people of only that state. Some state laws are about crime. Some are about state roads, schools, and other services. The *licenses* for cars, drivers, and businesses come from state government, too.

The government of Washington State is like the national government in many ways. Both have three branches— executive, legislative, and judicial. Like the U.S. Congress, our state legislature has two parts—a Senate and a House of Representatives.

Washington's State Government

WORDS TO UNDERSTAND

bill
candidate
guilty
jury
legislator
license
pardon
political party
veto

◀ *Our state seal is used on important documents. What do the words say? What is the date on the seal? What happened that year?*

Electing Leaders

Our state's voters elect many more leaders of state government than they elect for the federal government. Voters here choose the head of state education, for example. They choose a leader in charge of state lands. They also elect the most important judges for the state. But federal judges and other leaders are chosen by the president.

State Legislative Branch

Voters elect state senators and state representatives to make state laws. The state Senate and House of Representatives meet each year in January. The session lasts about two to four months. Then the *legislators* go home.

Legislators study and vote on *bills.* These are written ideas that some people want to be made into laws. Legislators also set taxes and decide how state money will be spent. They vote on many other things, too.

A bill becomes a law if both the Senate and the House of Representatives vote for it and the governor signs it.

Photo by Richard Cummins

William O. Douglas

William Douglas had several hard things to overcome while he was still a young boy in Yakima. His father died. Douglas got a disease called polio that made it hard for him to walk. He fought the disease by taking long, slow, painful walks.

Douglas grew up and taught high school. Then he hitchhiked to law school in New York City and got there with only six cents in his pocket.

Douglas became a lawyer and then a judge. Later, he became a judge in the U.S. Supreme Court, where he served longer than any justice in history.

Douglas never forgot about Washington. He wrote about protecting our special state.

State Executive Branch

Our governor is the head of the state executive branch. Here are some of the jobs the governor does. These duties are listed in the Washington State Constitution:

- See that state laws are carried out.
- Suggest actions for the legislature to take.
- Sign bills into law or **veto** them. (The governor can also veto part of a law.) To veto a law is to turn it down.
- Command the state military.
- *Pardon* (excuse) criminals.

A great many people work in this branch of state government. Some build and repair state roads. Some collect tax money. People work in health and education. State police and park rangers also work for this branch.

State Judicial Branch

This branch includes our state courts and judges. These courts settle problems about the meaning of a state law. Courts also decide if a person is *guilty* of a crime.

What happens to a person who is arrested for a crime? You've probably seen this on television. The person goes to court along with his or her lawyer. A judge, and often a *jury,* listen to people who may know about the crime.

After everyone has been heard, the jury must decide if the person is guilty or not. If the person is found guilty of the crime, the judge decides if the person should pay a fine or go to jail.

There are different levels of courts. One court might handle traffic tickets or give fines for breaking local laws. People who commit more serious crimes must go to a higher court.

Washington's State Supreme Court is the highest state court. Today, there are different judges. You can see them on the Internet at www.courts.wa.gov/courts/supreme/bios

POLITICAL PARTIES

Political parties are groups of people who have a lot of the same ideas about government. Most people choose either the Democratic Party or the Republican Party. They are the two main parties in Washington and in the rest of the United States. There are other parties, too.

Political parties want members of their party to get elected to government jobs. The people in each party choose *candidates* and help them run for office. The parties raise money to buy TV and radio advertising, make posters, and help in many other ways. The candidates give speeches to try and get votes. On election day, people vote for the candidate they think will do the best job.

Jennifer Dunn is a Republican. She is one of our representatives to Congress in Washington, D.C.

During elections, watch for these two animals on signs and badges:
*The **elephant** is the symbol for the Republicans.*
*The **donkey** is the symbol for the Democrats.*

Memory Master

Lesson 3

1. Name two ways that Washington State government is like the federal government.

2. Name one way that it is different.

3. Who is the head of the state executive branch?

4. Name the three branches of state government and tell at least one job of each branch.

5. What is a political party?

6. What are the two main political parties in Washington and the rest of the United States?

Local Governments

WORDS TO UNDERSTAND
county seat
ordinance

Local governments build roads for cities, towns, and neighborhoods. State and Federal governments build larger roads and highways that cross our nation and state.

Lincoln County Courthouse, Davenport

Counties and County Seats

Legend
County Seat ●

Whatcom

Bellingham

Friday Harbor

Skagit

San Juan

Mount Vernon

Island

Coupeville

Port Angeles

Port Townsend

Clallam

Snohomish

Jefferson

Everett

Kitsap

Seattle

Port Orchard

Mason

King

Kittitas

Grays Harbor

Shelton

Montesano

Tacoma

Olympia

Pierce

Thurston

South Bend

Chehalis

Pacific

Lewis

Wahkiakum

Cowlitz

Cathlamet

Skamania

Yakima

Kelso

Klickitat

Clark

Stevenson

Vancouver

The centers of state and national government are called capitals. The center of county government is called the county seat.

Photo by Mike Green

COUNTY AND CITY GOVERNMENT

Because places have different needs, governments for smaller regions of the state are important. The main example is county government. Washington is divided into thirty-nine counties. Each has its own government at a town that is the *county seat*. Find yours on the map.

County governments make laws called *ordinances* and provide services for people in the county. They run police and fire stations and provide clean water. They hire people to collect the garbage and take care of county parks.

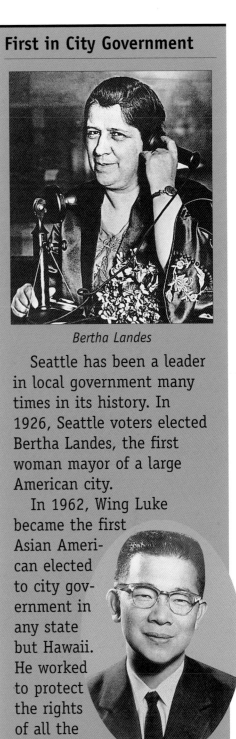

In some parts of Washington, towns and cities both provide these local services. If you live in one of these places, you are part of both a county government and a city government.

Local governments often pay for parks where you can play ball and have picnics. If you play soccer in a county park, you are using a county service. If you swim in a city pool, you are using your local city services.

Everyone is also part of a kind of local government called districts. For example, we all live in a school district, which runs the schools in our area.

Government for All of Us

Public schools are a service of local and state government. Your parents pay taxes to help pay for school buildings, books, paper, pencils, and teachers.

TAXES PAY FOR SERVICES

How do governments pay for these services? Taxes! You help pay, too. Every time you buy clothes or toys at a store, you pay a sales tax. Taxes come in many other forms. Here are some examples at each level of government:

- **Income tax**—People and companies pay a part of the money they make to the federal government.

- **Sales tax**—When you pay tax on something you buy, most of the tax money goes to the state.

- **Property tax**—County governments collect a tax on land, buildings, and homes.

Taxes Pay for Schools

One of the most important things taxes pay for is education. If you go to a public school, your school building, your books, and even your teacher are paid for with tax money. If you go to a private school, your parents have to pay for these things.

Lesson 4

Memory Master

1. What is the main kind of local government?
2. Give three examples of local government services.
3. How do governments pay for services?

Financing the State

Where the money comes from:

- Sales tax
- State property tax
- Business tax
- Federal government
- License and fees
- Lottery
- Other taxes

Where the money goes:

- Schools
- Health care
- Transportation
- Public safety
- Natural resources

Chapter 9 Review

Activity

Who Am I?

Read the clues and write the answers on a piece of paper. Then try making up more "What Am I?" puzzles for your friends.

1. I include the basic laws and ideas of Washington State government. What am I?

2. I tell why Americans wanted their own government. I was signed on July 4, 1776. What am I?

3. I am a branch of government with two parts: the Senate and the House of Representatives. Which branch am I?

4. I am the first ten amendments to the U.S. Constitution. I list the rights and freedoms that all Americans share. What am I?

5. I am a level of government. I include cities, towns, counties, and school districts. What am I?

6. I am a branch of government. I decide what laws mean and if they have been broken. Which branch am I?

7. I am the city where our state government leaders work. What am I?

Activity

Make a Book about Government

Why is government important? Make a book that tells some of the things you have learned in the chapter.

- Choose the topics you would like to include in your book, and make a page for each one.
- At the top of each page, write the name of the topic. Draw a picture and add some writing so others can learn about it, too.

Here are some examples you can use:

1. Laws

Making laws is one job done by governments. Laws tell people how they must behave. For example, today's laws say that children must go to school. They say that cars must stop at stop signs.

Laws help stop arguments. They help protect us and the things we own. The government hires police and other workers to make sure that laws are carried out.

2. Services

The local government provides services that our town needs, from schools to streetlights to clearing snow off our streets in the winter.

Geography Tie-In

1. On a wall map in your classroom, locate Washington, D.C., (our nation's capital) and Olympia (our state capital). Our representatives have to travel across the country to get to Washington, D.C.

   • About how many miles do our representatives have to travel to get to Washington, D.C.?

   • What kinds of transportation might our representatives use?

   • Choose two other states. How far do their representatives have to travel to get to Washington, D.C.?

2. Locate your county and county seat on the map on pages 198 and 199. Which counties are near yours?

0   500 Miles

Scale of Miles

Activity

Local Laws

Can you think of local laws, sometimes called ordinances, that affect you? They might have to do with speed limits, crosswalks, garbage pick-up, buses, or rules for your park.

   • Why do you think these laws were passed?

   • Which laws do you agree with?

   • Which ones would you like to change, and why?

   • What can you do when you think a law should be changed?

Most cities have an ordinance, or law, that says dogs must have a license and cannot run loose around the neighborhood.

Glossary

The definitions given here are for the **Words to Understand.** They are highlighted in yellow in the text. They are defined here the way they are used in this textbook.

A

advertising: promoting a product so people will buy it

agriculture: the business of raising plants and animals to sell for food

Allies: countries that fought the Axis powers in World War II

aluminum: a lightweight metal

amendment: an addition or change to a constitution

ancestor: a relative who lived before you

ancient: very old

apology: an expression of regret; to say you are sorry

apprentice: a person who learns a trade from a skilled worker

archaeologist: a scientist who studies clues to learn how people lived in the past

artifact: something made by people long ago

atlatl: a tool used to throw a spear

automobile: a car

average: between the highest and lowest

Axis powers: countries that fought the Allies during World War II

B

baby boom: a fast rise in the birth rate after World War II

bill: a written idea that people want to be made into law

botanist: a scientist who studies plants

brigade: a group of traders

button blanket: an Indian blanket that has designs outlined in buttons

C

canal: a waterway made by people; a natural, straight waterway

candidate: a person who seeks a public office

cannery: a business where food is put in cans

capital: the place in a nation or state where the central government is located

capital goods: goods that are already made and used to make some thing else

capitalism: an economic system of private ownership of business; competition in a free market

carnival: an outdoor event with rides and games

ceremony: a ritual; actions done the same way each time for a special purpose

challenge: to boldly go up against an idea or person; a hard task

citizen: a person who lives legally in a city, town, or country

Civil Rights Movement: an effort to gain equal rights for African Americans and others

civil war: when people in the same country fight against each other

climate: the weather in a place year after year

colony: a place under the control of another nation

communist: one who believes in communism (when government owns all land and businesses)

compete: to try to win; to gain advantage

compromise: where each side has to give up part of what they want in order to solve a problem

concentration camp: a prison camp for Jews in Europe during World War II

Congress: the branch of government that makes the laws

conserve: to use natural resources wisely

constitution: a document that gives the ideas and rules for government

consumer: a person who buys or uses things

continental climate: the climate far away from oceans, with hot summers and cold winters

continents: very large land areas almost surrounded by water

controversial: where there are opposing views

country: a land region under the control of one government

county seat: the town where county government is located

culture: the way a group of people lives

D

defeated: to lose; the side that lost the war

degree: part of a circle or globe

dense: thick

descendants: children, grandchildren, great-grandchildren, and so on

dictator: a person who can rule however he wants to

difficult: hard to do

discrimination: to treat other people badly just because they are different

disease: sickness

diverse: different; varied

document: an official paper

dynamite: an explosive

E

earthquake: a shaking or trembling of the earth

economic system: a country's way of making, buying, and selling goods and services

economics: the study of how people make, transport, buy, and sell goods and services

economy: the country's financial condition; how people earn and spend money

elect: to vote for a person

election: the process of voting people into office

elevation: how high the land is above the level of the ocean

elevator: a cage that moves people to different floors of a building

employee: a person who works for a company for money

entrepreneur: a person who has an idea and starts, owns, and runs a business

equator: an imaginary line around the middle of the earth; 0 degrees latitude

erode: to wear down rock with wind, water, or glaciers

erupt: to explode

expense: the cost; money spent

explorer: a person who goes to new places to learn about them

export: to ship out of the country

extinct: no longer existing

F

factors of production: things that must come together before something is sold

family crest: a design that tells a story in a family's history

federal government: government for all of the states

felt: made from pressed beaver hair and used to make tall hats

forestry: about forests

fossil: a remain or trace of an ancient plant or animal in rock

free enterprise: an economic system where people, not government, own and run businesses

freshwater: lakes and rivers that are not salty

G

general strike: when almost all workers in a city go on strike

generator: a machine that produces electricity

generous: to be giving

geography: the study of location, places, and cultures, and how they interact

geologist: a scientist who studies geology

geology: the study of the history of the earth as recorded in rocks

glacier: huge thick sheets of moving ice

gold rush: a time when thousands of people go to a place to find gold

goods: things that are made, bought, and sold

graffiti: writing or painting written illegally on public property

Great Depression: a time in the 1930s when many people were out of work

guilty: to be at fault

H

habitat: a natural place where plants and animals live together

harpoon: a spear used to hunt whales

headquarters: the place where the leaders work

hemisphere: half of the earth, usually divided by the equator or prime meridian

high-tech: dealing with advanced technology

Hispanic: a person of Latin American culture

Holocaust: the murder of Jews in Europe during World War II

homestead: to claim a piece of land, farm it, and own it for free after a certain number of years

human feature: changes that people make to the land such as farms, cities, bridges, or roads

hydroelectricity: electricity made by waterpower

I

immigrant: a person who comes to a new country to live

independence: freedom from another's control

inherit: to receive things or money from relatives who have died

internment camp: a U.S. prison camp for Japanese Americans during World War II

interpreter: a person who knows two or more languages and translates one to the other

interstate: a road that crosses many states

invention: a new creation that changes the way people live

irrigate: to water crops

J

jury: a group of people in a community who decide if a person is guilty of a crime

L

labor: the work people do

labor union: an organization of workers who try to get the business owner to give more pay and better working conditions

land region: a large region of land with mostly one kind of landform

landform: a natural land feature such as mountains, hills, plateaus, valleys, peninsulas, etc.

latitude: lines on a map that run east and west

lava: hot melted rock from inside the earth

legend: a story that tells about the past

legislator: a person in Congress who studies and votes for laws

license: a written permit to do something

local: close to home

longitude: lines on a map that run north and south

loss: in business, losing money instead of making it

M

marine climate: the climate near an ocean; a wet, mild climate

military: having to do with war

millionaire: a person who has a million dollars or more

mineral: a natural substance in the ground such as coal, gold, silver, salt, sand, stone, gas, etc.

minimum wage: the smallest amount of money that workers can be paid

minority group: a small part of a population that differs from the rest in some way

missionary: one who tries to convert others to his or her religion

moisture: water in the air

monopoly: when only one company produces a certain product

N

native: being born in a place; being naturally from a certain region

natural environment: the landforms, plants, and climate of a place

natural resource: something found in nature that people use, such as trees, water, minerals

New Deal: Roosevelt's plan to put Americans back to work and end the Great Depression

O

old growth forest: a forest with trees that are hundreds of years old

ordinance: a local law

orphanage: a place where children without parents lived
outhouse: an outdoor bathroom with a wooden seat over a hole
outnumber: to have more than the other side

P

pardon: to excuse people from crimes they commit
patriot: a person who loves his or her country
petroglyph: a rock carving
pioneer: a person who is among the first to settle a place
pirate: a person who robs ships
political party: an organized group of people who have the same ideas about government
pollute: to make the air or water dirty and unsafe
population: the number of people who live in a place
possession: something you own
potlatch: a Coastal Indian ceremony of feasting and gift-giving
powwow: a Native American festival with food, dancing, and contests
precipitation: water that falls to the earth as rain or snow
prejudice: to make judgments about people because of their race or religion
prime meridian: an imaginary line from pole to pole through England; 0 degrees longitude
product: goods; things that are made, bought, and sold
profit: the money earned after expenses are paid
Prohibition: a law that outlawed alcohol
protection: safety
protest: to complain against an action or idea
provide: to make available

R

recycle: to make into a new product; to use again in a new way
reform: a change in the way things are done; to make better
refugee: a person who seeks safety in another country
rendezvous: an event where trappers and Indians celebrated and traded furs and supplies
representative: a person elected to vote for other people
research: to learn by careful study
reservation: a piece of land set aside for Native Americans to live on
respect: to have high or special regard for a person
responsibility: a job or duty
restaurant: a place to sit down, eat, and pay for meals
riot: when a mob rebels in a violent way

S

salary: money paid to employees on a weekly or monthly basis
scientific: having to do with science; careful, orderly study
sea level: the average level of the ocean
segregate: to keep apart
service: in economics, something done for another person for money
shaman: a Native American spiritual leader who also healed the sick
shipyard: a place where ships are built
slavery: the practice of owning another person like property
spike: a long, thick nail used to build railroad tracks
steppe: dry, almost treeless land of grasses and low shrubs
stockade: a high log fence built around a fort
streetcars: long cars on tracks that moved people around in cities
strike: when all workers stop working so bosses will make things better on the job
suburbs: places outside the city where people live
supply and demand: when the selling price is affected by the amount available and the price people are willing to pay
surrender: to give up; to quit fighting a war
survey: to measure the land
symbol: a mark or design that stands for something else

T

teepee: a Native American home made of tall wooden poles and buffalo skins
territory: a region ruled by leaders appointed by the U.S. government; not a state
tide: the rising and falling of the ocean level, usually twice a day
totem pole: a carved wooden pole made by Native Americans to display family history
tourism: the industry of making money from people who visit
tourists: people who visit other places
trade: to buy and sell things with other countries
trading partners: those with whom we buy and sell
transportation: ways to move people or goods from one place to another
treaty: a formal agreement between two groups
tule: tall plants that grow wild in wetlands; cattails

U

union: an organization of workers who try to get better working
conditions and more pay

unique: to be different or special

unpopular: disliked

V

valuable: worth a lot; desirable

vegetation: plants

veteran: a person who served in the armed forces

veto: to say no to a bill; to prevent from becoming a law

volcano: hills or mountains from which lava and steam have erupted

W

wage: money paid to employees for each hour worked

wagon train: a group of wagons that followed one another

weir: a fence built across a stream so fish can be caught

wilderness: a place in its natural state where few humans live

Index

A

advertising, 168, 169
African Americans, 90, 119, 130, 142, 150, 152, 153
agriculture, 16, 17, 25, 178, *See also* farming
airplanes, 142, 149, 155, 156, 157, 163, 165
Alaska, 50, 64, 118, 122, 123
Alaska-Yukon-Pacific Exposition, 128
Aleutian Islands, 64
Allen, Paul, 173
Allies, World War II, 140
American Indians, *See* Native Americans
Appaloosa, 56
apples, 16, 178
archaeologists/archaeology, 41, 52
Asia, 27, 112, 180, 181, *See also* specific countries
atomic bomb, 141, 144, 154
automobiles, 121, 135
Axis powers, World War II, 140

B

Bainbridge Island, 143
Baldridge School, 95
Bauer, Eddie, 173
beavers, 72
Bellevue, 149
Bellingham, 30, 129
Bering Strait, 64
Bering, Vitus, 64
Bill of Rights, 193
bills, 195
Boeing Company, 156, 162-163, 165
Boeing, William, 133, 134
Bonneville Dam, 137
Bremerton, 175
British Columbia, 69, 72, 172
Britain/British, *See* England
buffalo, 55, 56
Bush, George and Isabelle, 90
Bush, President George W., 161
button blanket, 58

C

California, 106, 112, 113
camas, 54
Canada, 4, 26, 50, 69, 75, 99, 112, 116
capitalism, 164

Cascade Mountains, 12, 20, 23, 35, 43, 44, 53, 106, 113, 119
Catholic, 83, 86
cattle, 25, 172, 178
Cayuse Indians, 84
cedar, 47
Chin, Gee Hee, 172
China/Chinese, 112-113, 114, 150, 151, 152, 172, 174
city government, *See* local government
civil rights, 152
Civil War, 110, 130
Clark, William, 70-71, 73, 83, 99
climate, 12, 14
coal, 108
Coastal people, 43-45, 50, 54, 98
Cold War, 154
colonies, 186, 191
Columbia, 109
Columbia Plateau, 20, 24, 28, 53
Columbia River, 2, 10, 40, 54, 66, 67, 69, 71, 75, 138, 139, 176
Columbus, Christopher, 43
communist/communism, 154, 155
concentration camps, 141
Congress, 191, 195
Constitution, U.S., 188-189, 191, 193
Constitution, Washington State, 184, 195
consumers, 168
continents, 4, 5
Cook, Captain James, 65
county government, *See* local government
courts, 196
Curtis, Edward, 39

D

dams, 137, 138
Davenport, 184, 185, 198
Declaration of Independence, 186-187
democracy, 189
Democratic Party, 197
Denmark, 117
Denny, Emily Inez, 93
dinosaurs, 28
Douglas, David, 69
Douglas, William O., 196
Drake, Sir Francis, 63, 64
Dry Falls, 24
Dunn, Jennifer, 197
Du wamish, 43, 98

E

earthquakes, 35

S

Sacagawea, 71
Sager, Catherine, 85
salmon, 45, 46, 53, 174
Saloman, Edward, 117
Samoa/Samoans, 151
San Francisco, California, 106, 111
San Juan Islands, 69, 96, 151
Scandinavia, 117, 173
schools, 94, 95, 200, 201
Scotland, 69, 117
sea otters, 64
Sealth, Chief, 98
Seattle, 22, 35, 100, 101, 106, 111, 113, 115, 118, 122, 123, 128, 131, 133, 156, 158, 175, 176, 199
Seattle General Strike, 131
Seattle-Tacoma International Airport (Sea-Tac), 149, 177
segregation, 152
Senate/senators, 191, 195
September 11, 2001, 146-147, 161
shamans, 55
shipbuilding, 133, 142, 175
Skagit Valley, 178
slavery, 89
Snake River, 24, 176
Snipes, Ben, 172
Soviet Union, 62, 117, 140, 154
Spain/Spanish, 55, 62, 63, 69, 151
Spalding, Eliza and Henry, 83, 99
Spokane, 24, 30, 43, 55, 57, 83, 107, 115, 120, 129, 153, 158, 175, 177
state government, 189, 195-196
statehood, 115
Stevens, Isaac, 109, 110
strikes, 131, 166
Suquamish, 98
suburbs, 148, 149
supply and demand, 167
Supreme Court, U.S., 196
Supreme Court, Washington State, 196
Sweden, 117

T

Tacoma, 22, 30, 73, 106, 111, 113, 115, 129, 133, 175, 176
taxes, 200, 201
telephones, 120
televisions, 149
Thompson, David, 75
tides, 11, 45
totem poles, 50

tourism, 179
transportation, 10, 121, 176-177
trappers, *See* fur traders
Tri-Cities, 175, *See also* specific cities
Tyler, Jennie, 93

U

unions, 131, 166
U.S. Supreme Court, 196

V

Vancouver, British Columbia, 158
Vancouver, George, 68, 69
Vancouver Island, 67, 96
Vancouver, Washington, 86
Vietnam War, 155
volcanoes, 33
voting, 130, 194, 197

W

Wales, 117
Walla Walla, 101, 106, 108
Walker, Mary, 84
Washington, D.C., 187, 191
Washington, George, 186
Washington Territory, 109, 172
Wenatchee, 42
Western Lowlands, 20, 22
whales, 51, 52
Whitman, Marcus and Narcissa, 83-85, 86
Willamette Valley, 87
women's rights, 107, 130, 153
world fairs, 158
World War I, 133
World War II, 140-144, 148, 150, 151, 152

Y

Yakima, 121, 129
Yakima River, 24
York, 71

Credits

Amon Carter Museum 70 (painting, top)
Associated Press AP 51 (bottom)
Baker, Will 10 (bottom left)
Barrow, Scott 187
Benschneider, Ben 158 (top left), 159 (right)
Bergen, Joyce 40
Boeing Corporation 162-163, 165
Burke Museum of Natural History and Culture 38-39, 46 (top left)
Burton, Jon 171-172
Cheney Cowles Museum/Eastern Washington State Historical Society 107 (right), 138 (both), 139
Cheney Medical Archives 157 (right)
Clark, Wade Jr. 178 (bottom)
Cummins, Richard 17 (right), 30 (top), 50 (left), 73 (top), 179 (right), 195
Curtis, Edward 38-39
Curtis, Ashel 119
Crosetto, Maralyn 47 top
Della Piana, Leandro, 90 Courtesy of Open Hand Publishing
Fort Vancouver Historical Site 74 (bottom)
Glaze, Michael J. 23
Grant County P.U.D. 53 top
Green, Mike 13 (right), 17 (both top), 95, 139 (right), 198 (bottom)
Haight, Drury 84 (both)
Hilbert, Vi 55
Historical Society of Seattle and King County 126-127, 129 (bottom right), 133 (bottom), 134 (right), 141 (top), 199 (top)
Holman, Robert maps, charts, graphs
Hopkinson, Glen 80-81
Holocaust Memorial Museum 141 (bottom)
Idaho Dept. of Commerce and Development 106
Image Productions 200
Ivanko, John 16
Jackson, W. H. 77 (bottom)
Joslyn Art Museum 76 (both), 77 (top)
Kaufman, Steve 132 (top)
Levin, Mary 22 (top)
Library of Congress 70 (both left), 135 (left, right), 152
Lincoln County Historical Society 184-185
Los Angeles Dept. of Water and Power 112
Makah Museum 42 (right), 52
Mason, Mark 198 (top, both)
Microsoft Corporation 173 (bottom)
Miller, Alfred Jacob 76-77 (all)
Montana Historical Society 71 (inset)
Morgan, Dwight 178 (center)
Morris, LaVelle viii, 13 (left)
Murray, Barbara ix, 10 (top right)

Museum of History and Industry 100, 107 (left), 117, 131, 134 (left), 173 (center), 172 (bottom), 174
Myers, Susan 83, 87 (both)
National Park Service 45, 57, 68 (right), 155 (top)
National Archives 114 (bottom), 140, 144
North Wind 188
Office of the Governor 151 (right)
Ogle, Therese 69
Oltersdorf, Jim 25
Oregon Dept. of Fish and Wildlife 72 (left)
Oregon Dept. of Transportation 56 (top)
Oregon Historical Society 44, 54 (top left), 50 (right), 54 (top left), 63 (right), 66, 82
Pefley, Chuck 2-3, 22 (bottom), 24 (top right, bottom), 31
Pelz, Ruth 28
Peter Arnold, Inc. 132 (top)
Place, Chuck Cover, 21 (right)
Port of Seattle 10 (top left), 165 (bottom), 176 (both), 177
Rasmussen, Gary vi-vii (all), 12, 18-19, 42 (left), 48, 49, 130 (bottom), 167, 169
Rutz, Dean 35
Sauber, Kathy 157 (bottom), 177 (right)
Seattle Times, The 35, 146-147, 149, 153 (right), 154 (both) 156, 158 (top left), 159, 161
Seattle Aquarium 45 top, 46 (bottom), 64
Simon-Glaze, Shirlee 8 (right), 15 (top 3), 33
Sisters of Providence Archives, Seattle 86 (left)
Stevens, Otto 29
Stoffel, Keith 32
Stradling, Dale 24 (top left)
Till, Tom 21 (left), 34
University of Washington Libraries, MSCUA (Manuscripts, Special Collections, and Archives) 46 (top right), 50 (top), 54 (bottom), 60-61, 67 (both), 68 (top left), 74 (top), 75 (center), 94, 98 (bottom), 99, 101, 104-105, 109, 111, 112, 113 (both), 114 (top), 118 (both), 119, 122 (top), 128, 136, 142, 143 (both), 166 (top)
University of Washington News and Information 22 (top), 157 (bottom), 177 (right)
Utah State Historical Society 77 (bottom), 121 (bottom), 143 (right), 172 (left)
Vaughn, Greg 158 (bottom)
Wallace, Brian 47, 58
Walter, Sunny 8 (left), 15 (bottom)
Washington Dept. of Transportation 198 (top, both)
Washington Dept. of Tourism 41 (bottom)
Washington State Historical Society, Tacoma 50 (bottom), 123, 153 (center)
Washington State Office of Archaeology and Preservation 92 (top right, top left), 108 (bottom), 179 (bottom)
Weyerhaeuser 9
Whitman Mission National Historic Site 85
Wilcox, Bill 189
Wing Luke Asian Museum 199 (bottom)

All photos not listed are from the personal collections of the author or Gibbs Smith, Publisher.